WHAT CALVIN SAYS

AN INTRODUCTION TO THE THEOLOGY OF JOHN CALVIN

DEDICATION

To my wife Ann and my daughters Jennifer and Deborah. May "the Word of Christ," as so profoundly taught by John Calvin, "richly dwell within them."

WHAT CALVIN SAYS

AN INTRODUCTION TO THE THEOLOGY OF JOHN CALVIN

W. Gary Crampton

The Trinity Foundation
Jefferson, Maryland

Cover: This painting, found in a castle in 1955, had upon the back of it in French: Portrait of Calvin by Holbein. Hans Holbein (1497-1543) worked in Switzerland, Italy, France and the Netherlands, but is especially known as the court painter of King Henry VIII of England. Whether Holbein is actually the painter or not, the portrait is revealing. It gives the lie to the Calvin myth that he was austere and void of human affections. This is his youth with eyes that reveal rest and peace, eyes that are a doorway to a heart of gold.

© 1992 W. Gary Crampton

The Trinity Foundation
Post Office Box 700
Jefferson, Maryland 21755

ISBN: 0-940931-35-4

CONTENTS

FOREWORD

Who is John Calvin?

Ernst Renan, the nineteenth century French historian, thought he was "the most Christian man of his age."

Will Durant, the twentieth century American historian, thought Calvin "darkened the human soul with the most absurd and blasphemous conception of God in all the long and honored history of nonsense."

The nineteenth century English preacher, Charles Haddon Spurgeon, wrote that "the longer I live the clearer does it appear that John Calvin's system is the nearest to perfection."

The twentieth century American televangelist, Jimmy Swaggart, thinks that "Calvin has . . . caused untold millions of souls to be damned."

The eighteenth century French political philosopher Montesquieu thought that the people of Geneva "should bless the birthday of Calvin."

The nineteenth century German historian Leopold von Ranke thought Calvin was "the virtual founder of America."

The twentieth century *Oxford Dictionary of the Christian Church* calls Calvin "the unopposed dictator of Geneva."

Hated and loved by many, John Calvin remains, after 450 years, one of the most controversial figures of church history. His influence on Western civilization has been spectacular. The German sociologist Max Weber traced the rise of capitalism to

Calvin in his 1905 book, *The Protestant Ethic and the Spirit of Capitalism.*

More recently, in *The Interaction of Law and Religion,* Harold Berman has written: "Calvinism has also had profound effects upon the development of Western law, and especially upon American law. The Puritans carried forward the Lutheran concept of the sanctity of individual conscience and also, in law, the sanctity of individual will as reflected in property and contract rights. . . . Seventeenth century Puritans . . . laid the foundations for the English and American law of civil rights and civil liberties as expressed in our respective constitutions: freedom of speech and press, free exercise of religion, the privilege against self-incrimination, the independence of the jury from judicial dictation, the right not to be imprisoned without cause, and many other such rights and freedoms. We also owe to Calvinist congregationalism the religious basis of our concept of social contract and government by consent of the governed."

But far more important than these political, economic, and social consequences of Calvin's thought is the role he played in the recovery and propagation of the Gospel of Jesus Christ, which had been all but eclipsed by the superstitions and hegemony of the Roman church. For a thousand years Europe had been shrouded in theological darkness; only a few dim lamps of truth flickered in the night.

Then, in the early sixteenth century a brilliant dawn came; an Augustinian German monk defied the Pope and the totalitarian church-state that had repressed truth, freedom, and Christianity for a millennium. Calvin, 26 years younger than Luther, enlightened by God, became a Christian, a Lutheran, and turned his brilliant mind to writing a summary of Christian doctrine. His *Institutes of the Christian Religion* became the manifesto of the Reformation. An indefatigable preacher and writer, Calvin turned Geneva into the arsenal of Christianity, flooding Europe and the world with tracts, books, sermons, and missionaries. Perhaps at no time since the first Christian century had the world seen such a rapid spread of Christianity.

What makes Calvin important to history and to us is not the events of his life, but his ideas. Calvin himself would be the first to admit that his ideas are not original, but taken from the Bible. Trained in both philosophy and law, Calvin digested the Scriptures and created an elegant system of theology, a system that has been rejected as "too logical" by those uncomfortable with some of Calvin's conclusions. Calvin was a clear and logical thinker and writer, and his *Institutes of the Christian Religion* remains one of the masterworks of Christian theology.

In this book, Gary Crampton has distilled Calvin's theology and explained it for the modern reader. It is our hope, however, that the reader will not use this book as a substitute for reading Calvin, but simply as an introduction to Calvin's works. Those who have not yet read Calvin have a feast awaiting; this book is simply the hors d'oeuvres.

John W. Robbins
October 15, 1992

JOHN CALVIN: A CHRONOLOGY

1509	Born July 10 in Noyon, France.
1528	Received a Master of Arts degree from the University of Paris.
1531	Obtained Doctor of Law degree; his father died.
1532	Wrote his first book: *Commentary on De Clementia.*
1532-34	During this time Calvin was converted (probably during 1533).
1533	Joined the Reformation in Paris.
1534	Wrote his first theological work: *De Psychopannychia (On the Sleep of the Soul).*
1536	Published the first edition of *The Institutes of the Christian Religion* in March.
1536-38	Encounter with William Farel: first Geneva period.
1538-40	Calvin was banished from Geneva and went to Strasbourg as pastor.
1539	Completed the second edition of *The Institutes.*
1540	Married Idelette de Bure in August. Published his *Commentary on Romans..*
1541-64	Second Geneva period.
1549	Calvin's wife died.
1559	Final edition of *The Institutes.* Calvin became a citizen of Geneva. Academy was established.
1564	Died in Geneva, May 27.

CHAPTER ONE

THE MAN, THE CHURCHMAN, AND THE STATESMAN

Introduction

John Calvin is one of Christendom's greatest thinkers. His writings include commentaries, sermons, letters, essays, tracts, and a systematic theology. The *Corpus Reformatorum* contains fifty-nine volumes of Calvin's *Works*. A whole system of religious thought bears his name: Calvinism. John Calvin was, of course, not the author of this system of dogma; he was merely one of its finest advocates.

Surprisingly, many Christians know very little about Calvin, the man and his theology; too few understand what Calvin says. It is the purpose of this little book to change this situation. What John Calvin has to say can contribute significantly to contemporary Christian thinking.

The Man

John Calvin (Jean Chauvin) was born July 10, 1509, at Noyon in Picardy, France. He was the second of five children of Gerhard Chauvin, a man of some means, who was the secretary of the Bishop of Noyon. Thus, he was able to obtain certain

1

privileges for his son. For example, young John became a chaplain at the age of twelve, an office which he later exchanged for a higher paying position. Before Calvin was a teenager, the Reformation in Germany, led by Martin Luther (1483-1546), was already in full swing.

Calvin's mother, Joan France (Jeanne Lefranc), died when he was young. After her death John, at the age of fourteen, was sent to the University of Paris to study for the priesthood. He received a Master of Arts degree in 1528. Calvin's practical father demanded that he take up the study of law, due to its potential monetary rewards.

The son dutifully followed his father's advice, and in 1531, the year of his father's death, he obtained his doctorate of law. Calvin then returned to Paris, seeking to become a classical scholar. His first book, *A Commentary on De Clementia* of Seneca, appeared in 1532. Calvin was an exceptionally well read scholar. Even after his conversion, he never denied the benefit of reading the works of some non-believers. The Lord, said the Reformer, had given them skills (*e.g.,* in the area of the liberal arts and sciences) from which God's children could benefit; but great care was always to be exercised in reading their works.[1] In his *Commentary* on Titus 1:12, for example, Calvin writes, "All truth is from God; and consequently, if wicked men have said anything that is true and just, we ought not to reject it; for it has come from God" (see also his *Commentary* on Genesis 4:20). Of course, one could distinguish between truth and falsehood only by knowing Scripture.

Sometime between 1532 and 1534, John Calvin became a Christian. In his own words, "God by a sudden conversion subdued and brought my mind to a teachable frame" (Preface to the *Commentary* on Psalms). In 1534, he surrendered his clerical offices, which had been used to fund his education. Some view this as a sure sign of his conversion. It was in this year that he wrote his first theological work: *De Psychopanny-chia (On the Sleep of the Soul),* a polemic against the "soul sleep" doctrine of certain Anabaptists.

While in Paris, Calvin had made friends with Nicolas Cop, who later became Rector of the University of Paris. In 1533, Cop made his All Saint's Day address, in which he called for a more "spiritual" church. The speech was not well received by the Roman Catholic Church. In the address, which Calvin probably authored, Cop advocated the principles of the Reformation. Because of this, both Cop and Calvin had to flee for their lives. (The Roman Catholic Church would later declare Calvin to be "the most daring, subtle, adroit, [and] successful enemy of the church of God [*i.e.,* Rome].")[2] Calvin went to Basel, Switzerland, where he studied early Christian theology.

John Calvin certainly understood the need for reformation of the church. This is evidenced by his 1539 *Reply to Cardinal Sadolet.* According to this reply, reform was no longer possible under the Church of Rome. And, stated Calvin, he was ready to lay down his life for Reformational truth. Luther called this *Reply* "a writing which has hands and feet."[3]

After his conversion, John Calvin committed himself to a study of the Scriptures. *Sola scriptura* was for him the way of life. The power of the Word of God overwhelmed the Reformer. Later in his *Institutes* (I:8:1), Calvin wrote:

> Now this power which is peculiar to Scripture is clear from the fact that of human writings, however artfully polished, there is none capable of affecting us at all comparably. Read Demosthenes or Cicero; read Plato, Aristotle and any others of that tribe. They will, I admit, allure you, delight you, move you, enrapture you in wonderful measure. But betake yourself from them to this sacred reading [*i.e.,* Scripture]. Then, in spite of yourself, so deeply will it affect you, so penetrate your heart, so fix itself in your marrow, that, compared with its deep impression, such vigor as the orators and philosophers have will nearly vanish. Consequently, it is easy to see that the Sacred Scriptures, which so far surpass all gifts and graces of human endeavor, breathe something divine.

According to Philip Melanchthon, who became a life-long friend of the Reformer, Calvin became "the Theologian" of the Reformation.[4] He began writing his *Institutes of the Christian Religion* in Basel, and completed the first edition in 1536, at the age of twenty-seven. This work, an instant success, was addressed to Francis I, King of France, as a defense of the Christian faith.

The *Institutes,* a treatise on systematic theology, was Calvin's *magnum opus.* It became his life-work; that is, for nearly a quarter of a century, Calvin refined, expanded, revised, and re-organized this summation of Reformed theology. The final edition, published in 1559, was five times the size of the original.

In the words of Benjamin B. Warfield of Princeton Seminary, "the *Institutes* lies at the foundation of the whole development of Protestant theology."[5] Indeed, says Warfield, "What Thucydides is among Greeks, or Gibbon among eighteenth-century English historians, what Plato is among philosophers, or the *Iliad* among epics, or Shakespeare among dramatists, that Calvin's *Institutes* is among theological treatises."[6]

Calvin's *Commentaries* cover the entire New Testament, except for 2 and 3 John and Revelation; the Old Testament works include all but the Solomonic, and some of the historical books. Not only was John Calvin "the Theologian" of the Reformation, he was also its finest expositor of Scripture.[7]

Calvin left Basel after completing the *Institutes.* He intended to go to Strasbourg, Switzerland, where with his family's wealth to finance him he hoped to lead the quiet life of a scholar, studying and writing. Due to the warfare between Francis I and the Emperor Charles V, he had to take a detour and spend one night in Geneva. There he was met by Reformer William Farel (Calvin's elder by some twenty years) who, by means of threatening God's condemnation upon the tranquil life of the scholar, persuaded Calvin to stay in Geneva for the cause of the Reformation. Farel bluntly stated, "I speak in the name of Almighty God. You make the excuse of your studies. But if you yourself refuse to give yourself with us to this work of the Lord, God will curse you, for you are seeking yourself rather than Christ."[8] The young Calvin said that he was "stricken with terror," as if the "hand of God from heaven" were there arresting him.[9] The younger man became the elder's assistant.

Calvin and Farel soon encountered strong opposition from the government of Geneva. The government insisted on the state's right to administer discipline within the church as well as within the civil sphere. Calvin and Farel strongly disagreed; the church, they maintained, is a separate institution, and is to administer its own discipline, in accordance with the Word of God. The opposition was so strong that in 1538 Calvin and Farel were forced out of Geneva. Calvin headed for Strasbourg. There he met Martin Bucer (to whom he was greatly indebted for theological insight on various subjects), lectured on theology, and took on the ministry of a French refugee church.

Calvin remained in Strasbourg for three years. In 1540, at the age of thirty-one, he married the widow of a former Anabaptist, Idelette de Bure, who had two children at the time. She died nine years later. Calvin greatly mourned the loss of "the best companion of my life."[10] Idelette had given him three children, all of whom died in infancy.[11]

While in Strasbourg, Calvin expanded his *Institutes,* wrote his *Commentary* on the book of Romans, as well as the previously mentioned *Reply to Cardinal Sadolet.* In 1541, the church in Geneva begged him to return as one of its pastors. He did so with reluctance, knowing of the hardship that awaited that calling. But, with the conviction that it was God's will for him to do so, he went as "a sacrifice to the Lord."[12] He remained in Geneva until his death on May 27, 1564.

From 1541 to 1555, Calvin experienced great opposition to his attempts at reform. But from 1555 until his death he was considerably more successful. Calvin believed, says Frank Roberts, that God "intended to establish a holy commonwealth on earth."[13] He worked hard toward that end. He taught that the church and state must work together for the furtherance of God's Kingdom. Each sphere was separate, but under God's law.

The Genevan church was structured along the lines of Calvin's 1537 *Ecclesiastical Ordinances*. Basically, a Presbyterian form of government was established. There was the company of pastors, the consistory (pastor and elders), the school (for teaching of children; Calvin wrote his first catechism, *Instruction in the Faith*, for the education of the youth), and Geneva Academy (university level training). Theodore Beza, Calvin's successor at Geneva, was the first rector of the Academy.

The liturgy for worship was outlined in Calvin's *Form of the Ecclesiastical Prayers and Hymns*. His *Geneva Catechism* also played a key role in the life of the church. John Knox could later call Geneva "the most perfect school of Christ that ever was in the earth since the days of the apostles."[14]

Toward the end of his life, Calvin's health, which was seldom good, deteriorated. For a period of time he had to be carried to the Cathedral to preach. His devotion never waned. Up to the end he sought to read, study, and teach the Word of God. He was truly, as Jean Cadier so aptly said, "a man God mastered."[15] His symbol was an outstretched hand holding a burning heart, offered up to God; his motto, "My heart, O Lord, I offer as a sacrifice to God—promptly and sincerely."[16] At Calvin's death, by his own instruction, he was buried in an unmarked grave.

The great significance of the man John Calvin is recognizable by the influence which his teaching has had on Western history and culture. Gregg Singer writes:

> Calvinism has had a greater influence on human history and institutions than any other theology ever formulated by the church. . . . It provided a *weltanschauung*, a world and life view, by which the Reformed faith could be translated into every phase of human life.[17]

Politics, economic thought and practice, philosophy, and education have all been influenced by John Calvin.

According to Singer, the numerous national creeds and confessions which emerged from Calvin's doctrine speak to the far-reaching effects of the Reformer's work. There is the Gallic Confession (1559), the Scottish Confession (1560), the Belgic Confession (1561), the Thirty-Nine Articles of Religion (1563), the Heidelberg Catechism (1563), the Second Helvetic Confession (1566), and the Westminster Standards, consisting of the Confession of Faith and the Larger and Shorter Catechisms (1643-1648). Of the Westminster Standards Singer says:

> [In these the] theology of Calvin reached its classic creedal expression, and they have remained unsurpassed in the history of the church in their fidelity to biblical truth, in their profundity of thought and clarity of expression. Even three hundred years later they stand as an enduring landmark of the Reformed faith to the English speaking world.[18]

The great nineteenth century Reformed Baptist evangelist Charles Spurgeon wrote, "no age before him [Calvin] ever produced his equal, and no age after him has seen his rival."[19] The eighteenth century Reformed theologian Francis Turretin maintained that "John Calvin was a man whose memory will be blessed in every succeeding age. He instructed and enlightened, not only the church of Geneva, but also the whole Reformed world."[20]

The Churchman

John Calvin was a strong churchman. He firmly believed in the holy universal church (the communion of saints). The church was the mother of all believers, in that the saints are nourished and built up by and through the ministry of the church (*Institutes,* IV:1:1-5).

Calvin's view of church government was Presbyterian. He regarded himself as a fellow elder with the other presbyters (*Institutes* IV:4:1-4). He believed that the chief calling of the pastor and teacher was the ministry of the Word of God. He wrote, "it was a principle of long standing in the church that the primary duties of the bishop [Calvin believed "bishop" and "elder" were synonyms] were to feed his people with the Word of God, or to build up the church publicly and privately with sound doctrine" (IV:4:3). The pastors were also to administer the sacraments and visit the congregational members when needed (IV:4:3; IV:1:22).[21]

Calvin was noted for his humility, teachableness, willingness to forgive those who had wronged him, and quickness to ask forgiveness of those whom he had wronged. He attracted friends readily; and during his life of Christian service, he formed some very close relationships. His numerous extant letters reflect the fact that he looked to some of these for comfort and advice. He was also a very sensitive person. It is said that when his friends rebuked him, or when he became aware of their displeasure with him, Calvin was deeply hurt, sometimes even to the point of becoming ill over these matters. In short, Calvin had a heart for the people of God; he was capable of manifesting great love and compassion.[22]

Calvin sought the peace of the church. According to Francis Nigel Lee, "he was the living embodiment of Augustine's ideal for the church: 'In fundamentals—unity; in non-essentials—diversity; in all things—charity.' "[23] Calvin was never willing to compromise biblical principles to attain any goal. Professor Dorner writes, "Calvin was equally great in intellect and character, lovely in social life, full of tender sympathy and faithfulness to friends, yielding and forgiving toward personal offences, but inexorably severe when he saw the honour of God obstinately and malignantly attacked."[24] In a personal letter to Ami Perrin, Calvin wrote, "You yourself know . . . that I am one to whom the law of my heavenly Master is so dear that the cause of no man on earth will induce me to flinch from maintaining it with pure conscience."[25]

Calvin was ardently opposed to the false doctrines of the Roman Catholic Church, the Anabaptists, the Libertines, and others. He argued against them in both his preaching and writing. For example, in 1545 he wrote the tract *Against the Fantastic and Raging Sect of the Libertines*.[26] He strongly warned against all forms of ungodly alliances: marital, ecclesiastical, and national.

At the same time, Calvin had his shortcomings. He, like Luther, manifested a fiery temper; he was naturally choleric. To a complaint by Martin Bucer about this very weakness, Calvin replied, "My struggles are not greater against my vices, which are very great and numerous, than against my impatience; and my efforts are not wholly useless. I have not, however, been able yet to conquer that ferocious animal."[27] In his *Sermons* on 1 Timothy (3:1-4), he refers to himself as a "ferocious wild beast."

As a pastor and teacher, Calvin was an example of true godliness. He is renowned for his piety. "True piety," says Calvin, "consists . . . in a sincere feeling which loves God as Father as much as it fears and reverences Him as Lord, embraces His righteousness, and dreads offending Him worse than death."[28]

In the words of Robert Peterson:

> Calvin was a pastoral theologian. It was in the midst of intense Christian service in Geneva that he perfected the *Institutes* and wrote the commentaries. It is therefore not surprising that his theology tugs at the heart, as well as challenges the mind. . . . Calvin calls us to both intellectual integrity and practical application.[29]

According to Calvin, the whole Christian life can be summarized by self-denial: a total resignation of each and every part of one's life to the sovereign will of God (*Institutes* III:7:1-10). In this act of self-denial, a part of which is cross-bearing, the Christian is to manifest moderation (in food, drink, etc.) and modesty (in dress, lifestyle, use of wealth, etc.), while continually meditating on the future life (III:8,9).

Calvin was very much a man of prayer. He called prayer "the principal exercise which the children of God have"; it is a "true proof" of saving faith (*Sermons* on 1 Timothy 2:1,2). Calvin himself was a disciplined "pray-er." He practiced and recommended regular times of prayer: (at least) when rising in the morning, when retiring at night, and at meals (*Institutes* III:20:50). Such good habits are hard to break.

But by no means could Calvin be called an ascetic. He was no pietistic escapist, retreating from the world. He writes, "We are nowhere forbidden to laugh, or to be satisfied with food, . . . or to be delighted with music, or to drink wine" (*Institutes* III:19:9).

Calvin was also an evangelist. He took advantage of every opportunity to present Christ to the lost. He would frequently distribute tracts in the market place. He even sought to evangelize the blasphemer Servetus up to the day of his death. And of all the Reformers, Calvin was the one most interested in missions.

The Statesman

Calvin believed that the Bible alone is the Word of God, the only rule for each and every area of life. The role of social institutions was to be determined by nothing other than Holy Scripture. In the words of Ronald Wallace:

> He [Calvin] was convinced that the challenge and power of the gospel must be allowed to cleanse, regenerate and direct not only the human heart but every aspect of social life on earth— family affairs, education, economics and politics. Christ sought not only an altar in the human heart for His priestly ministry, but a throne at the centre of all human life for His kingly ministry.[30]

As to the doctrine of the state, or civil magistrate, Calvin attempted to form a God-centered commonwealth on earth. His theology taught him that this was no option; it was a divine mandate (*Institutes* IV:20:1-30). He recognized the various forms of civil government: absolute monarchy, aristocracy, and democracy; and he opted for aristocracy—a form of republican government.

He considered the office of civil magistrate the highest of all callings (*Institutes* IV:20:4). The state, as a God-ordained institution, was to enforce the whole of the Decalogue in its duties (IV:20:2,6). Further, the civil magistrate must be obeyed by the citizens of the land, until it forbids them to do what God commands, or commands them to do what God forbids (IV:20:23-25).

Calvin held to a biblical distinction and separation between church and state, but not a separation that removed the state from its biblical setting. The difference was one of function, not of authority. According to Singer, "Calvin believed that both the church and the state are divinely ordained and created, and that both are directly under Jesus Christ, who is both Lord of the church and King of kings." These two institutions are assigned to two different spheres of operation, and both are still under God's law.[31]

According to Calvin, a Christian economy was one that would operate under the economic system of biblical capitalism. Communism was condemned by the Reformer. Calvin strongly encouraged the establishment of business enterprises in Geneva, while at the same time encouraging charity to those in need.[32] The very fact, said the Reformer, that God is the one that causes some to be rich, is the reason that the rich should be charitable in giving to the poor (*Commentary* on Deuteronomy 8:17; *Sermons* on Deuteronomy 15:11-15).

In a Christian society, men are allowed and encouraged to pursue wealth in a godly fashion. Proper biblical investing was encouraged. "Money," said Calvin, "in itself is good" (*Com-*

mentary on Matthew 19:4). Calvin distinguished between loans to the poor and needy, in which no interest was to be charged, and business loans, in which it was permissible to receive a fair market interest (*Commentary* on Exodus 22:25; Ezekiel 18:1-9). The poor and afflicted (not the sluggards) were to be cared for by the ministry of the church. Deacons were to assist in this task (*Institutes* IV:3:8,9). But there was no thought of a program to redistribute wealth.

The Protestant "work ethic" was developed from Calvin's teaching.[33] A man's vocation in life was God-given; it was to be viewed as his "holy" calling from God (*Commentary* on 1 Corinthians 7:18-24). Even the homemaker, as she labors in her kitchen, is to do so to the glory of God (*Sermons* on Ephesians 6:5-9). Thus, all legitimate types of work are sacred, and man is to work hard in his calling. Calvin himself was a tireless worker; his days began at 5 a.m. and sometimes lasted far into the night. But the chief purpose of work is not to become wealthy. True reward from godly labor was spiritual and moral (*Commentary* on Psalm 127:2; Luke 17:7).

Calvin taught that education should be God-centered.[34] Education was the duty of the parents, not the state (*Commentary* on Deuteronomy 6:6). The purpose of education is to bring mankind to a knowledge of God's truth in every field of study. Languages, logic, math, music, rhetoric, and poetry were all taught at the Academy, as well as theology. God's Word, of course, is to be foundational in each discipline. The Bible functioned as "the spectacles" through which all is to be viewed (*Institutes* I:6:1). As man further studied and learned about the universe in which he lived, he would be better equipped to glorify his Maker. His God-centered learning would also make man a better citizen.

According to Calvin, the family was the chief institution in God's economy.[35] Hence, it was imperative to maintain proper family relationships. The husband was the head of the family; the wife was to be submissive to him; and the children were to obey both their father and mother. The chief calling of the woman was that of wife, mother, and homemaker. She was not to hold office in the church or in civil government; to do so would undermine the familial structure ordained by God (*Commentary* on 1 Timothy 2:11-15).

Although Calvin saw that there was a proper place within a Christian setting for biblical "family planning," he favored large families (*Commentary* on Psalm 127:3-5). He, along with Luther, denied any inherent virtue in celibacy. Marriage and family were the normal state for both men and women (*Commentary* on Genesis 2:18-25). He taught that divorce, although not the ideal remedy in marital relations, is permissible for adultery and irreconcilable desertion (*Commentary* on Deuteronomy 24:1-4).

CHAPTER TWO

CALVIN ON KNOWLEDGE

John Calvin begins his theological masterpiece, *The Institutes of the Christian Religion*, with these sentences: "Nearly all the wisdom we possess, that is to say, true and sound wisdom, consists of two parts: the knowledge of God and of ourselves. But, while joined by many bonds, which one precedes and brings forth the other is not easy to discern" (I:1:1). Without a knowledge of one's self, there is no knowledge of God. But to know one's self (and the whole world in general), there must first be a knowledge of God. God is known both better, and before, oneself or anything else (I:1:1-3).

Calvin begins his *Institutes* with epistemology (the theory of knowledge); he does not begin with how we know there is a god, and then go on to seek to prove that this god is the God of Scripture. His starting point is revelation. The doctrine of God follows epistemology (I:13ff.). Calvin maintains that there is a two-fold revelation of God to man: general (I:3-5) and special (I:6-12). The former is general in audience (all mankind) and limited in content; the latter is more restricted in audience (those who read the Bible) and much more detailed in content. The latter is now found in Scripture alone. Further, general and special revelation are in perfect harmony (I:10:1).

In a spectacular and thoroughly Biblical reversal of traditional philosophy and theology, Calvin teaches that God—not one's self or the world—is the object best known to man.

15

General Revelation

Calvin taught that the Spirit of God has implanted an innate knowledge of God in all men, a knowledge which is propositional and ineradicable. "There is within the human mind, and indeed by natural instinct, an awareness of divinity. This we take to be beyond controversy. . . . God Himself has implanted in all men a certain understanding of His divine majesty" (*Institutes* I:3:1). Man, as the image bearer of God, even has the moral law imprinted in his heart: "it has been engraven by God in the minds of men" (IV:20:16). B.B. Warfield correctly maintains that for both Calvin and Augustine the innate knowledge in man lies at the root of all of his knowledge of God; here man has inborn propositional revelation.[1]

This innate knowledge enables man to see the rich revelation of God in creation. "Wherever you cast your eyes, there is no spot in the universe wherein you cannot discern some sparks of His glory. . . . There are innumerable evidences both in heaven and on earth that declare His wonderful wisdom" (*Institutes* I:5:1,2). All men have knowledge of God which leaves them without excuse (I:3-5; *Commentary* on Romans 1:18-21; 2:14,15).

Nevertheless, due to the effects of sin on the mind, fallen man, even though he possesses this seed of true religion, continually suppresses the knowledge which he has and knows to be true (*Institutes* I:3-5). "But although we lack the natural ability to mount up unto the pure and clear knowledge of God, all excuse is cut off because the fault of dullness is within us. And, indeed, we are not allowed thus to pretend ignorance without our conscience itself always convicting us of both baseness and ingratitude" (I:5:15). Without the "spectacles" of the propositional truth of God's Word, sinful man is not able to come to a sound and saving knowledge of God (I:6:1).

It can be seen that although Calvin did adhere to natural or general revelation (in contrast to Karl Barth, for example), he did not develop a natural theology. He teaches that the divinely implanted (and propositional) knowledge of God and (because of this) the daily disclosure of God's power in nature are more than sufficient to prove the God of Scripture to be the one and only true God (*Institutes* I:3-5). Calvin speaks of the persuasiveness of the religious and/or moral argument (I:3:1,2; I:5:8-10), the cosmological argument (I:5:6; I:16:8,9), the argument from common grace (I:5:7), and the argument from the human anatomy (I:5:2,3), but unaided by Scripture, these all speak in vain (I:5:14). Not even the knowledge of the resurrection of Jesus Christ led the disciples to faith; it merely confirmed the faith they already possessed (II:2:2-5). Calvin writes, "The proofs of faith must be fet from [sought at] the mouth of God alone. If we dispute about matters which concern men, then let human reasons take place; but in the doctrine of faith, the authority of God alone must reign, and upon it we must depend" (*Commentary* on Acts 17:2). In other words, one does not attempt to prove God; he is the necessary premise of all proof, the object of knowledge better known than any other.

Special Revelation

John Calvin taught that the propositional truth of special revelation is necessary if one is going to come to a saving knowledge of God through Jesus Christ. General revelation reveals God as creator; Scripture alone reveals him as Savior (*Commentary* on Romans 1:16,17).

Calvin writes:

> Scripture, gathering up the otherwise confused knowledge of God in our minds [*i.e.*, innate knowledge], having dispersed our dullness, clearly shows us the true God. This, therefore, is a special gift [*i.e.* special revelation], where God, to instruct the church, not merely uses mute teachers but also opens His own most hallowed lips. Not only does He teach the elect to look

upon a god, but also shows Himself as the God upon whom they are to look. . . . God has provided the assistance of the Word for the sake of all those to whom He has been pleased to give useful instruction, because He foresaw that His likeness imprinted upon the most beautiful form of the universe would be insufficiently effective . . . . We must come, I say, to the Word, where God is truly and vividly described to us from His works (*Institutes* I:6:1,3).

True knowledge, says Calvin, "is that which is delivered to us by the law and the prophets" (*Commentary* on Jeremiah 44:1-7).

The Geneva Reformer maintains that Scripture is self-authenticating and self-evident (*Institutes* I:7:5). There are, says Calvin, numerous evidences, both internal and external, that the Bible is God's infallible revelation to mankind. There is the antiquity of the Bible (I:8:3,4), various miracles and prophecies (I:8:12), and the faithfulness of the martyrs (I:8:13). But apart from the inner testimony of the Holy Spirit, these evidences are "vain"; they are "secondary aids to our feebleness" (I:8:13; compare I:7:1-5).

Calvin would have been in perfect agreement with the Westminster Confession of Faith (I:4-5):

The authority of the Holy Scripture, for which it ought to be believed and obeyed, depends not upon the testimony of any man or church, but wholly upon God (who is truth itself) the author thereof; and therefore it is to be received, because it is the Word of God. . . . We may be moved and induced by the testimony of the church to an high and reverent esteem of the Holy Scripture; and the heavenliness of the matter, the efficacy of the doctrine, the majesty of the style, the consent of all the parts, the scope of the whole (which is to give all glory to God), the full discovery it makes of the only way of man's salvation, the many other incomparable excellencies, and the entire perfection thereof, are arguments whereby it does abundantly evidence itself to be the Word of God; yet notwithstanding, our full persuasion and assurance of the infallible truth and divine authority thereof is from the inward work of the Holy Spirit bearing witness by and with the Word in our hearts.

Calvin did not attempt to prove by extra-biblical arguments that the Bible is the Word of God.[2] He writes, "They mock the Holy Spirit when they ask: Who can convince us that these writings came from God? Who can assure us that Scripture has come down whole and intact even to our very day? . . . Thus, the highest proof of Scripture derives in general from the fact that God in person speaks in it. The prophets and apostles do not boast either of their keenness or of anything that obtains credit for them as they speak; nor do they dwell upon rational proofs. Rather, they bring forward God's holy name, that by it the whole world may be brought into obedience to Him" (*Institutes* I:7:1). Therefore, it is "not right to subject it [the Bible] to proof and reasoning" (I:7:5). The Bible is the axiom on which all knowledge and proof are based.

Calvin is not anti-logic. Philip Schaff claims that, as the best theologian and exegete of the Reformation period, Calvin, "never abused reason . . . but assigned it the office of an indispensable handmaid of revelation."[3] Rather, it is unaided human thinking that Calvin opposes (*Institutes* I:5:14). This is confirmed by church historian C. Gregg Singer. Singer claims that although Calvin never wrote much on philosophy, he nevertheless did advocate the legitimacy and necessity of a Biblical philosophy. In fact, he laid the groundwork for a solid Reformed Christian philosophy based solely on the Word of God.[4] Calvinists historically have been characterized as being too logical, rather than anti-logical.

Although there is a common ground between believers and non-believers, due to the fact that they all are created by God, there are no notions common to Christianity and secular philosophy (*Institutes* I:5:13). True faith rests alone on an implicit belief in the Word of God, as revealed by the Holy Spirit (III:2:6-10). Calvin says that evidentialistic apologetics—trying to prove the existence of God and the truth of the Bible—is "doing things backwards" (I:7:4).

How then, according to Calvin, does man come to the knowledge of God? He doesn't. Man innately knows God. Knowledge of God is possible and inescapable because he has chosen to reveal himself to man. Such knowledge is not derived by either sensation or reasoning. Knowledge is revelational and propositional, and its source is God.

Further, says Calvin, Jesus Christ is the one who makes all knowledge possible. He is the eternal *Logos.* Christ makes knowledge possible and inescapable because he is "the true light which gives light to every man coming into the world" (*Commentary* on John 1:9,14,17).

CHAPTER THREE

CALVIN ON SCRIPTURE

After his conversion Calvin devoted his life to the study and exposition of Scripture. He was an advocate of *sola scriptura;* that is, he believed "the whole counsel of God, concerning all things necessary for His own glory, man's salvation, faith, and life, is either expressly set down in Scripture, or by good and necessary consequence may be deduced from it."[1] Calvin's voluminous writings—commentaries, sermons, and catechisms—fully attest to this fact. Scripture, to John Calvin, is "the Word Of God," which comes to us from "the mouth of God" (*Institutes* I:7:1,5).

Further, we have seen that Calvin taught that Scripture was necessary for salvation. That is, sin is so pervasive in fallen man that God's general revelation is continually suppressed. If men were taught only by general revelation, "they would hold to nothing certain or solid or clear-cut, but would be so tied to confused principles as to worship an unknown god" (*Institutes* I:5:12). Thus, God has given us His Word, as "spectacles" to direct us to the Savior (I:6:1). According to Calvin, the Holy Spirit is the effectual agent, which united with the Word, as the instrumental, objective factor, gives light to a sin-darkened mind (II:2:20).[2] The Spirit causes the sinner to believe what he reads.

This Word also is that sole source of truth through which man is to interpret all of the world. In other words, Scripture, as God's Word, is sufficient. It is not only that which reveals Christ as Savior, it is also the one and only guide for the Christian's life (*Institutes* I:6:1,2). Calvin's high view of Scripture is particularly evident in his refutation of certain anti-Trinitarian heresies of his day:

> Let us use great caution that neither our thoughts nor our speech go beyond the limits to which the Word of God itself extends. And let us not take it into our heads either to seek out God anywhere else than in His sacred Word, or to think anything about Him that is not prompted by His Word, or to speak anything that is not taken from that Word. But if some distinction does exist in the one divinity of Father, Son, and Spirit—something hard to grasp—and occasions to certain minds more difficulty and trouble than is expedient, let it be remembered that men's minds, when they indulge their curiosity, enter into a labyrinth. And so let them yield themselves to be ruled by the heavenly oracles [*i.e.*, Scripture], even though they may fail to capture the height of the mystery.[3]

Inspiration

Calvin maintained that all sixty-six books of the Old and New Testaments were fully inspired by God in the original manuscripts (*Institutes* I:8:10). The Bible is the Word of God; it does not "become" the Word of God, as in neo-orthodoxy.[4] Scripture, says Calvin, was written through God's prophets and apostles, who were moved along by the Holy Spirit, so that they wrote without error. These men were the "certain and authentic amanuenses of the Holy Spirit and therefore their writings are to be received as the oracles of God" (*Institutes* IV:8:9). "We have received it [the Bible] from God's own mouth by the ministry of men. . . . [In the Bible] we hold the unassailable truth" (I:7:5).

Therefore, Scripture is to be given the same reverence which one owes to God himself, "since it has proceeded from Him alone, and there is nothing human mixed with it" (*Commentary* on 2 Timothy 3:16). The Bible owes its origin to the Triune God (*Institutes* I:6:1-3). It is his "eternal and inviolable truth"; God speaks in his Word (I:7:1). In the words of William Wileman, "the Word of God was as sacred to him [Calvin] as if he heard it spoken by the lips of its Author."[5]

Calvin's view of inspiration maintains that the authors of Scripture were acted upon by the Holy Spirit in an "organic" way, in accordance with their own personalities, characters, temperaments, gifts, and talents. Each author wrote in his own style, and all the while it was the Holy Spirit moving him to write infallible truth. In fact, each author's style was itself produced by the providence of God.

It is true that the Reformer uses the word "dictated" when referring to the inspiration of Scripture (*Commentary* on 2 Timothy 3:16). But, as B.B. Warfield concludes, this usage in Calvin speaks to the result, not the mode, of inspiration; that is, "the production of a pure Word of God free from all human admixtures."[6] With this conclusion, E.J. Young is in complete agreement. Young writes:

> At the same time, although the term dictation in itself is not objectionable and expresses forcefully the Divine origin of the words of the Bible, it is perhaps unwise to use the word today without some qualification. A new connotation has come upon the term which it obviously did not have in the day of Calvin. When we speak of dictation, there immediately comes to mind the thought of the businessman dictating a letter to his stenographer, or the teacher dictating an exercise to her pupils. In both these instances it does not make too great a difference who takes down the dictation. One stenographer can probably do it as well as another, and if one is not available, another can easily be obtained. Likewise, when the teacher dictates a passage to her class, the important thing is that the pupils take down precisely what has been dictated, and do not add to it or

subtract from it. The person of the stenographer or of the pupil is in reality a comparatively negligible factor. Such, however, is not the situation with respect to the human writers of the Bible. True enough, the words which they employed were taught them by the Holy Spirit, but it is not the case that it makes no difference who wrote those words. It is not true that Peter might just as well have written the Pauline epistles as the great Apostle himself. It would serve the interests of clarity, therefore, if, in the discussion of this doctrine, we lay stress upon the fact that although the Bible teaches that its very words are from God, it most emphatically does not teach a mechanical dictation view of inspiration.

Men like Turretine, Calvin and others who have written on this subject have been as eager to do justice to the human side of the Bible as have some of the modern rejectors of the biblical doctrine. It is a sad thing that scholarly men of our day constantly erect a straw man and seek to attack it instead of coming to grips with the Scriptural teaching itself. Those who believe the Bible and who wish to do justice to its teaching are as concerned as anyone to refute the notion that inspiration was a mechanical kind of dictation, that the human writers were mere automata whose personalities were entirely suspended in the writing of the books of the Bible.[7]

To Calvin, it is not merely the doctrine and/or the content of biblical revelation that is inspired; it is the Scripture itself. Every word is God-breathed (*Commentary* on 2 Timothy 3:16 and 2 Peter 1:20,21). This is the doctrine of plenary, verbal inspiration.[8]

Authority

According to Calvin, the authority vested in Scripture is derived from its unique origin.[9] The sixty-six books of Holy Writ are not only the sole authority for the church of Jesus Christ, but they are also the sole authority for every institution (*Institutes* I:7:1,2; II:7:6-17; *Commentary* on Isaiah 30:1). Singer maintains that it was Calvin's high view of Biblical revelation by which he could "with full assurance assert that the Scriptures are the final authority in all areas of human life."[10] It is the inner testimony of the Holy Spirit which corroborates this authority (*Institutes* I:7:1-5). "Those who are inwardly taught by the Holy Spirit acquiesce implicitly in Scripture" (I:7:4). Non-believers can have a certain understanding of Scripture, but because they are not "inwardly taught" by the Spirit, they never have a genuine spiritual grasp of it (*Commentary* on James 2:19 and 1 Corinthians 2:14).

As the inner testimony of the Holy Spirit is necessary to confirm the authority of God's Word and to cause one to spiritually acquiesce to it, Calvin also recognizes our need for the Spirit to further illuminate the Word of God for us. In this process, the Spirit does not reveal new information which causes the reader to believe and/or further understand the Scriptures. Rather, the Spirit progressively gives to the Christian a greater and greater understanding of the Scriptures. He sheds more light on the biblical texts so that the believer can more fully grasp the fullness of the message set forth in the Bible. The Christian's mind is transformed to think and act biblically (*Commentary* on Romans 12:1,2; 2 Peter 1:19-21; Hebrews 5:12-14).

Calvin did not adhere to any form of extra-biblical special revelation (*e.g.*, prophecy and tongues).[11] That is, the canon was closed at the end of the apostolic age, so that God now speaks authoritatively in his written Word alone. (The canonicity as well as the authority of Scripture depends on divine inspiration.) The New Testament documents are the "limits of revelation" (*Commentary* on 1 Peter 1:25). Writes Calvin, "God will not speak intermittently through some and through others; nor will He add prophecies to prophecies, or revelations to revelations. Rather, He has so fulfilled all functions of teaching in His Son that we must regard this as the final and eternal testimony from Him. In this way, the whole New Testament time, from the point that Christ appeared to us with the preaching of His gospel even to the Day of Judgment, is designated by 'the last hour' . . . 'the last times' . . . 'the last days.' This is done that, content with the perfection of Christ's teaching, we may learn not to fashion anything new for ourselves beyond this or to admit anything contrived by others" (*Institutes* IV:8:7).

The Charismatic camp cannot claim the Genevan. His basic position was that God does not reveal himself to man (in special revelation) apart from Scripture. According to Calvin, "We cannot expect revelation to come through heavenly oracles or private communications or visions or irregular signs, since the days for such modes of communication are long past."[12]

John Murray aptly sums up Calvin's view of biblical authority:

> The sum of this is clear. God speaks in Scripture. In it He opens His sacred mouth. In Scripture the majesty of God confronts us. The divinity inheres in the Scripture and it therefore exhibits the plainest evidence that it is God's Word. When we bring sound minds it compels our submission and obedience. And our conclusion must be that this is but another way of saying that Scripture is by its nature divinely authoritative.[13]

The Word Preached

For John Calvin, the preaching of the Word out of the mouths of God's ministers, is, when properly spoken, to be considered as nothing less than the Word coming out of the mouth of God, because he "employs [such] men as His ministers" (*Commentary* on Isaiah 55:11). In this sense, "the Word of God is not distinguished from the word of the prophet" (*Commentary* on Haggai 1:12). It is, of course, the Spirit united with the Word that empowers the preaching. "All power of action . . . resides in the Spirit . . . and thus all power ought to be entirely referred to God alone" (*Commentary* on Ezekiel 2:2).

When the Word is biblically preached, it is a sign of the presence of God and the instrument of Christ's rule. The Spirit continues to speak through his Word in this God-ordained function. The Lord approaches his people through the preaching of Scripture (*Commentary* on Isaiah 50:2). "God has ordained His Word as the instrument by which Jesus Christ, with all His graces, is dispensed to us."[14]

Further, says the Reformer, the gospel is the sceptre for Christ's Kingdom; he rules his church by means of it (*Commentary* on Hosea 1:11). Moreover, it is also the means by which Christ intends the reconciliation of the whole world; that is, the restoration of all things, in Christ (*Commentary* on Isaiah 51:16). According to Calvin, when the Word of God is preached it has a two-fold effect: it either softens or hardens the heart (*Commentary* on 2 Corinthians 2:14-17). It always accomplishes its purpose. "As the Word is efficacious for the salvation of believers, so it is abundantly efficacious for the condemning of the wicked" (*Commentary* on Isaiah 55:11).

The Interpretation of Scripture

With this in mind, it should be no surprise to learn that Calvin considered sound exegesis, *i.e.,* faithful biblical interpretation, as imperative. He was a scholar of extraordinary measure; he was well read in all fields. He used "the best tools and methods of scholarship available at his time."[15] In the words of John Murray, "Calvin was the exegete of the Reformation and in the first rank of biblical exegetes of all time."[16] Singer calls him "the prince of expositors."[17]

The way one seeks God is by giving himself to a serious study of the Word (*Commentary* on Genesis 48:15). True biblical interpretation will lead one into a deeper relationship with Jesus Christ. "The Scriptures should be read with the aim of finding Christ in them" (*Commentary* on John 5:39). When the Bible is faithfully interpreted, the Spirit so works that Scripture shows forth Christ (*Institutes* I:9:3).

Calvin relied heavily on both Augustine and John Chrysostom in his studies. The former was by far the most influential on the Genevan (Calvin quotes Augustine over four hundred times in the *Institutes* alone). Calvin referred to Augustine as the most biblical of all of the Church fathers.[18] Along with Augustine, Calvin was devoted to the basic hermeneutical principle of "the analogy of faith"; that is, Scripture is its own best interpreter (*Commentary* on Romans 12:6; *Institutes* IV:27:32).

Yet Calvin takes issue with Augustine in opposing any form of allegorical interpretation. He avoided speculative theology altogether. At one point he writes:

> [T]he Bible was not given to us to satisfy our foolish curiosity and pride. Yet Paul says it is useful. For what? To instruct us in sound doctrine, to comfort us, to inspire us, and to make us able to perform every good work. If anyone asks us what constructive power we expect to receive from it, the answer can be given in one sentence, that through it we learn to place our trust in God and to walk in fear of Him.[19]

Further, in his *Commentary* on Romans 9:14 he states, "When the Lord closes His holy mouth, let us also stop the way, that we may not go further."

In all of his exegesis Calvin had a genuine desire to edify the church. In his Dedicatory to the exposition of the minor prophets he writes:

> If God has endued me with any aptness for the interpretation of Scripture, I am fully persuaded that I have faithfully and carefully endeavoured to exclude from it all barren refinements, however plausible and fitted to please the ear, and to preserve genuine simplicity, adapted solidly to edify the children of God, who, being not content with the shell, wish to penetrate to the kernel.[20]

As to his own ministry of the Word, John Calvin was an arduous laborer. In addition to his preaching each and every Lord's Day, he preached each Thursday in the university, and gave a public exposition every Friday. This, of course, was in addition to his writing ministry, which was extensive. The man seemed to possess an indefatigable industry.[21]

Scripture as a Means of Grace

Calvin, along with the other Reformers, considered the Scriptures, together with the sacraments (and prayer), as a means of grace. The "means of grace" are those means by which the Spirit of God ministers to the saints, building them up in the faith. These means, according to Calvin, are indispensable to the sanctification of the Christian.

The Word of God functions in this way in that it is the "spiritual food of the soul," which must not be neglected; in the Word Christians see the face of Christ, and are renewed (*Institutes* IV:1:5). God comes to meet with his saints in his Word; it is through the Word that the blessings of God's promises flow to the elect (*Commentary* on Psalms 18:31; 81:14, and 119:65).

The Christian man, says Calvin, loves the Word of God. It is an "unfeigned love of God's law [which] is certain evidence of adoption, since such love is the work of the Holy Spirit." One who despises the Word reveals a hardened heart; to despise the Word is tantamount to despising God himself (*Commentary* on Psalms 119:159; 95:8). When the law of God is written in the heart by the Spirit, that law will rule the individual. His life will be conformed to God's Word through the process of sanctification (*Commentary* on Jeremiah 31:33).

The Law of God

Historically, Reformed theology has not greatly separated the law and the gospel, though each is carefully distinguished from the other. Law without gospel is merely a dead letter, but there is no gospel without the law that reveals one's need for the grace of God in Christ (*Commentary* on 2 Corinthians 3:4-18).

In his *Institutes* and other writings, Calvin distinguished categories of the law: moral (II:8:1-59), civil (II:7:10,11; IV:20:14,15), and ceremonial (II:7:1,2,16,17). His overall teaching confirms that the moral law (*i.e.,* the Ten Commandments and the general equity of the civil law of Israel) was continually binding on all mankind. Here he would have been in basic agreement with the Westminster Confession of Faith (XIX:4, 5):

> To them [the people of Israel] also, as a body politick, He [God] gave sundry judicial laws, which expired together with the state of that people, not obliging any other now, further than the general equity thereof may require. . . . The moral law doth for ever bind all, as well justified persons as others, to the obedience thereof. . . . Neither doth Christ in the gospel any way dissolve, but much strengthen this obligation.

Calvin, for example, was convinced that the civil magistrate is obliged to enforce both tables of the Decalogue. Not to do so was to disobey the God of the law. The state was to prevent open idolatry, swearing and cursing, illicit forms of dance, and Sabbath disobedience, as well as promote proper marital relationships, sanctity of human life, etc. It was to work toward that holy commonwealth which God intended to establish on earth.

Frank C. Roberts writes:

> Building upon the doctrines of God and predestination, Calvin developed an activistic form of Protestantism quite unlike that of Luther. Both Luther and Calvin believed that a

sovereign God would certainly accomplish his purposes in the world. But Luther tended to limit his interest in this work of God to personal salvation, while Calvin believed God also intended to establish a holy commonwealth on earth. In Geneva, Calvin attempted to found such a commonwealth which would honor God in every area of life.[22]

That Calvin was a strong advocate of the civil law is related by Philip Schaff:[23]

Calvin's plea for the right and duty of the Christian magistrate to punish heresy by death stands or falls with his theocratic theory and the binding authority of the Mosaic code. His arguments are chiefly drawn from the Jewish law against idolatry and blasphemy, and from the examples of the pious kings of Israel.

In his *Sermons* on Deuteronomy, Calvin's strong adherence to the binding nature of the general equity of the Mosaic law is abundantly obvious.[24]

As for the ceremonial law:

Christ by His coming has terminated them [the ceremonies], but has not deprived them of anything of their sanctity; rather, He has approved and honored it. Just as the ceremonies would have provided the people of the Old Covenant with an empty show if the power of Christ's death and resurrection had not been displayed therein; so, if they had not ceased, we would be unable today to discern for what purpose they were established (*Institutes* II:7:16).

Calvin also taught that the law of God has a three-fold purpose:

1. pedagogical or educational (*Institutes* II:7:6-9): the law shows the righteousness of God and discloses the sinfulness of man, leading him to seek God's forgiveness;

2. political (II:7:10,11): the law restrains sin, sinners, and criminals, and is to be used to protect the community against unjust men;

3. pattern or model (II:7:12,13): the law is a pattern for life.
It admonishes the Christian man to seek and obey his God. This
third use of the law is the principal use in Calvin's theology. It
not only reveals the character of God (II:8:51), it also sets forth
his will (II:8:59). In the law God "lays down what He demands
from us, and, in short, everything necessary to be known"
(*Commentary* on Isaiah 8:20). It is "the everlasting and
unchangeable rule to live by" (*Institutes* II:7:13).

CHAPTER FOUR

CALVIN ON GOD

The doctrine of God, writes Singer, is central to Calvin's thought, "simply because it is central to the Scriptures which reveal Him. If Lutheranism found its center in the problem of man's salvation, Calvinism, on the other hand, looks primarily to the glory of God as its focal point: man's chief end is to glorify God and to enjoy Him forever."[1]

Calvin, in a letter to Cardinal Sadolet, writes that a man's thoughts must never be confined to matters regarding himself; rather, the prime motive of man's existence is to be found in a "zeal to illustrate the glory of God. For we are born first of all for God, and not for ourselves. As all things flowed from Him, and subsist in Him ... they ought to be referred to Him."[2] Calvin, as with other systematic theologians, studies the doctrine of God with regard to his being (*Institutes* I:13) and his work (I:14-18). In both he is fully in accord with the Westminster Standards.

The Being of God

Calvin nowhere goes into a lengthy explanation of the attributes of God. But in the *Institutes*, in the section on the knowledge of God (I:1-12), he briefly discusses some of his "perfections," his "powers," and his "excellencies." Calvin does this by means of contrasting the God of Scripture with the heathen gods (I:10:1-3). Here he speaks of God's goodness, righteous vengeance, patience, mercy, justice, truthfulness, etc. Such divine attributes should lead man to fear, trust, worship, and yield to God (I:10:1,2). In his 1536 *Confession of Faith*, Calvin writes, "Following, then, the lines laid down in the Holy Scriptures, we acknowledge that there is only one God, whom we are both to worship and serve, and in whom we are to put all our confidence and hope: having this assurance, that in Him alone is contained all wisdom, power, justice, goodness and pity."[3]

We can say with all confidence, through a study of his sermons, commentaries, tracts, treatises, and his *Institutes*, that Calvin would have given full approval to the Westminster Shorter Catechism's definition of God: "God is a Spirit, infinite [*i.e.*, omnipresent], eternal, and unchangeable in His being, wisdom, power, holiness, justice, goodness, and truth."

Further, Calvin frequently refers to the "glory" of God. This glory is not found within the Reformer's various lists of God's attributes, but it is associated with his "majesty." It is manifested in all of his works, but most particularly it is seen in Christ. Calvin viewed the glory of God as nothing other than "the intrinsic Godness of God," which is inherent in the perfections essential to him as God.[4]

The Trinity

The God of Scripture, states the Reformer, is monotheistic and trinitarian. He is one in essence, yet three in persons; each person is one hundred percent deity (*Institutes* I:13:1-20). In this sense the God of Scripture is distinguished from all idols (I:13:2). Calvin writes:

> There are in God three hypostases [persons] . . . the Father

and Son and Spirit are one God, yet the Son is not the Father, nor the Spirit the Son, but . . . they are differentiated by a peculiar quality. . . . [W]here simple and indefinite mention is made of God, this name pertains no less to the Son and the Spirit than to the Father. But as soon as the Father is compared with the Son, the character of each distinguishes the one from the other. . . . [W]hatever is proper to each individually, I maintain to be incommunicable because whatever is attributed to the Father as a distinguishing mark cannot agree with, or be transferred to, the Son (*Institutes* I:13,2,5,6).

Within the Trinity there is a perfect unity, a unity taught in both the Old and New Testaments. Calvin approvingly quotes Gregory of Nazianzus as saying, "I cannot think of the one without quickly being encircled by the splendor of the three; nor can I discern the three without being straightway carried back to the one" (*Institutes* I:13:17).

According to the Geneva Reformer, the doctrine of the Trinity, in its magnificent unity, is perfectly logical. In his *Catechism of the Church of Geneva* we read:

Master: Since there is no God but one, why do you here mention three, the Father, Son, and Holy Spirit?

Scholar: Because in the one essence of God, it behooves us to look on God the Father as the beginning and origin, and the first cause of all things; next the Son, who is His eternal wisdom; and, lastly, the Holy Spirit, as His energy diffused indeed over all things, but still perpetually resident in Himself.

Master: You mean then that there is no absurdity in holding that these three persons are in one Godhead, and God is not therefore divided?

Scholar: Just so.[5]

In Calvin's doctrine of God there is no room for subordinationism (the doctrine that there is one God, who is the Father; the Son and the Spirit are lesser gods, if gods at all) or modalism (the doctrine that God is one in essence and one in person; there are not three persons, there are merely three ways of referring to the one person) within the Trinity. In fact, he maintains that these two pseudo-doctrines are the root of all heresy (*Institutes* I:13:21-29). (Calvin's definition of a heretic is one who holds to a false doctrine and is unteachable [I:13:21-22].) In this section of the *Institutes* Calvin is overly gracious in supporting some of the early church fathers (*e.g.*, Tertullian, Justin), whom he claims were not confused in their Trinitarianism. At the same time, he correctly cites Augustine's pure orthodoxy in this matter. (It must be remembered that even though Calvin will frequently appeal to the teachings of other theologians, the Bible alone is the standard by which all dogma must be tested.)

Calvin does properly recognize an order of economy, or administration, within the Triune Godhead. Here there is a form of subordination. It is the Father who sends the Son and the Father and Son who send the Spirit to carry out their individual tasks in redemption (*Institutes* I:13:6,24,26,28). Calvin is not happy with the terminology of the "eternal begottenness" or "eternal generation" of the Son (and thus, by implication, the "eternal procession" of the Spirit), if one is referring to the ontological Trinity. (He is militantly opposed to the implicit subordinationism expressed in the Nicene creed: "begotten out of the Father," "out of *[ek]* the being *[ousias]* of the Father.") This is a "foolish doctrine," says Calvin; it is "of little profit" and "burdensome" to speak of the Son's ontological relationship with the Father in this manner (*Institutes* I:13:29); it is a "detestable" doctrine (I:13:24). Of course, if this language is used with regard to the Son's economic relationship to the Father, then it is perfectly proper.

Calvin also readily affirms that the term *begetting* is proper if all we refer to is the eternal relationship that the Son has with the Father. The Son has always been the Son (God is immutable); he derives his Sonship from the relationship in which he stands with the Father (*Institutes* I:13:7,8,18,23,24). Calvin writes:

> [W]e teach from the Scriptures that God is one in essence,

and hence that the essence both of the Son and of the Spirit is unbegotten—but inasmuch as the Father is first in order . . . He is rightly deemed the beginning and fountainhead of the whole divinity. . . . Likewise we confess that the Son, since He is God, exists of Himself, but not in respect of His person; indeed, since He is the Son, we say that He exists from the Father. Thus His essence is without beginning; while the beginning of His person [*i.e.*, with respect to order] is God Himself (I:13:25).

But this is a wholly different thing than ascribing ontological derivation to the Son.[6]

In his *Institutes,* Calvin argues for the full deity of the Son (I:13:7-13) and the Spirit (I:13:14,15) as well as that of the Father. As to the former, Calvin cites numerous Old Testament passages to support Jesus' preincarnate existence (Isaiah 9:6; Jeremiah 23:5,6; Judges 6:11,12,20-22). And in the New Testament the titles and names referring to deity are used of Christ. Likewise, the works performed by the Son confirm his divinity (I:13:7-13). Further, in his *Commentaries* on Romans 9:5, Titus 2:13, Hebrews 1:8, and 1 John 5:20, Calvin teaches that the Bible refers to Christ as true God.

As to the Holy Spirit, his deity is also manifested in the Old as well as the New Covenant. His works (*e.g.*, creation) are set forth as those of a divine being. Likewise, both the Old and the New Testaments clearly reveal his salvific labors, his authorship of Scripture, his indwelling of the elect, etc. The very fact that blasphemy of the Spirit is an unforgivable sin likewise manifests his deity (*Institutes* I:13:14,15).

The Works of God

The Westminster Shorter Catechism (Q.7) states that the works of God are determined by his eternal decrees: "The decrees of God are his eternal purpose, according to the counsel of his will, whereby, for his own glory, he hath foreordained whatsoever comes to pass." And further (Q.8), that the works can be summarized under two main headings, creation and providence: "God executes his decrees in the works of creation and providence." With these two statements Calvin is in perfect agreement.

According to the Genevan Reformer, nothing in the universe occurs by chance. There are, in actuality, no contingent events; there is no such thing as luck or fate (*Institutes* I:16:2-4; *Commentary* on Joel 2:11). All things that have ever taken place, or that ever will take place, come as a result of God's sovereign decretive will. His will is the first cause, the governing factor of all things (*Commentary* on Genesis 25:29; Daniel 4:34). Commenting on Daniel 4:34, Calvin writes:

> [W]e must learn what the true praise of God really is; namely, when reduced to nothing, we acknowledge and determine all things to be according to His will; for, as we shall afterwards see, He is the Governor of heaven and earth, and we should esteem His will as the source of law and reason, and the final appeal of justice.

Moreover, in his *Institutes* (III:23:2), Calvin asserts:

> God's will is, and rightly ought to be, the cause of all things that are. For if it has any cause, something must precede it, to which it is, as it were, bound; this is unlawful to imagine. For God's will is so much the highest rule of righteousness that whatever He wills, by the very fact that He wills it, must be considered righteous. When, therefore, one asks why God has so willed, you are seeking something greater and higher than God's will, which cannot be found.[7]

God's sovereign decretive will extends to the election of some and the reprobation of others before the fall; it thus includes the fall of man. In the *Institutes* (III:23:7), the Reformer refers to the doctrine of predestination as "an awe-inspiring" decree. Like the Westminster Assembly after him, Calvin claims that although this "awe-inspiring" doctrine needs to be proclaimed, it needs to be "handled with special prudence and care"[8] (*Institutes* III:21:1).

Further, in his *Commentary* on Malachi 1:2-6, Calvin states:

> We now see how the folly of those vanishes away who would have foreknowledge to be the cause of election; and also that they who murmur against God are sufficiently refuted by this reason, that it is in His power either to choose or to reject, inasmuch as He is under obligation to none. . . . As to reprobation, the cause of it is sufficiently manifest in the fall of Adam, for, as we have said, we all fell with him. It must be observed that the election of God is anterior to Adam's fall; and that hence all we who are rescued from the common ruin have been chosen in Christ before the creation of the world, but that others justly perish. . . .

In a letter to Philip Melanchthon Calvin wrote, "The doctrine of the gratuitous mercy of God is entirely destroyed unless we hold that the faithful whom God has thought fit to choose out for salvation are distinguished from the reprobate by the mere good pleasure of God."[9] In complete agreement with Augustine, Calvin maintains that "election could not stand except as set over against reprobation" (*Institutes* III:23:1).

In his *Commentary* on Deuteronomy 29:29, Calvin makes the classical Reformed distinction between the decretive and the preceptive will of God. The decretive will (God's decrees) determines what must happen; the preceptive will (God's commands) is the law which men are obliged to obey. God's decretive will is hidden in the mind of God; it is absolute and determined by him alone; it is not for man to know unless God reveals it. The preceptive will, on the other hand, is revealed in Scripture. It is that will of God for man by which he is to live. Hence, it is for us and our children to know. Man is held accountable for his disobedience to the preceptive, not the decretive, will. Man cannot disobey God's decretive will, for God is sovereign.

Creation

Calvin taught that the origin of the universe is given to us in the first two chapters of the book of Genesis. This includes the creation of the world (*Institutes* I:14) and man (I:15). It is by his Word that God spoke the universe into existence, and all to display his grace and glory (I:14:22). Too, all three members of the Godhead played an active role in the creation: "God [the Father] by the power of his Word and Spirit created heaven and earth out of nothing" (I:14:20).

Calvin maintained that the creation of the world occurred in a period of six days (*Institutes* I:14:2). He would have nothing to do with a day-age or a literary framework theory. Interestingly, in the sixteenth century the question seems to have been, "why did not God create the world in a moment of time, rather than in six twenty-four hour days?" Today, of course, the question is one of an old earth versus a young earth; not so in the days of the Reformer. Calvin, along with the majority of the church, held to a very young earth (I:14:1).

Further, says Calvin, the world was created *ex nihilo* (out of no pre-existent material). He states, "That we may apprehend with true faith what it profits us to know of God, it is important for us to grasp first the history of the creation of the universe, as it has been set forth briefly by Moses. . . . God by the power of His Word and Spirit created the heaven and earth out of nothing" (*Institutes* I:14-20). Not only this, says the Reformer, but the earth is the center of the universe (*Commentary* on Genesis, Argument section). Moreover, the creation of the world and all things therein is for God's own glory.

The creation of the universe included the creation of angelic beings (*Institutes* I:14:5-19), as well as mankind (I:15). As to the latter, man is the "noblest" of all creatures, made in the image of God (I:15:1-8), with a body (the physical element) and soul (or spirit) (the non-physical element). Man, as God's image bearer, is to show forth the glory of God (I:15:3,8). Although the whole man is to reflect God's glory, the non-physical element is superior to the physical, in that it is immortal. God's image "mainly" rests in the non-physical part of man; herein is the "primary seat" of the divine image. The spiritual element of man, then, is superior to the physical (I:15:2,3).[10]

The image of God, which rests "mainly" in the non-physical element of man (*Institutes* I:15:3), is two-fold. That is, man is both metaphysically and ethically God's image bearer (I:15:3-5). As to the former, man is a spiritual, moral, rational, immortal being. This part of the image is defaced, but not effaced, by the fall. As to the latter, man possessed true knowledge, holiness, and righteousness (Ephesians 4:24; Colossians 3:10). This part of the image was eradicated by the fall, and can only be restored through the grace of Christ (I:15:4).

Providence

For Calvin, the doctrines of creation and providence are inseparable; he is no deist. He writes:

> To make God a momentary Creator, who once for all finished His work, would be cold and barren, and we must differ from profane men especially in that we see the presence of divine power shining as much in the continuing state of the universe as in its inception. . . . Faith ought to penetrate more deeply, namely, having found Him Creator of all, forthwith to conclude He is also everlasting Governor and Preserver—not only in that He drives the celestial frame as well as its several parts by a universal motion, but also in that He sustains, nourishes, and cares for, everything He has made, even to the least sparrow. . . . All parts of the universe are quickened by God's secret inspiration (*Institutes* I:16:1).

Further, Calvin states:

> Herein lies the unfathomable greatness of God: not only did He once create heaven and earth, but He also guides the whole

process according to His will. Thus he who confesses God as
Creator, while supposing that He remains tranquilly in heaven
without caring for the world, outrageously deprives God of all
effective power.[11]

The providential work of God involves all three members
of the Trinity (*Institutes* I:13:12,14). Just as the world was
created by the powerful Word of God (Hebrews 11:3), so also is
it preserved and governed by that same Word (*Commentary* on
Hebrews 11:3).

In Calvin's theology there is a universal, or general, as well
as a particular, or special, providence of God (*Institutes*
I:16-18). The former has to do with the grace which is universal
to all mankind; the latter pertains only to the elect. Charles
Partee writes:

> Calvin considers God's work in the government of the
> world under three aspects. First, there is a universal operation by
> which God conducts all creatures according to the condition
> and properties which he gives to each of them when they are
> formed. This direction is called the order of nature. . . . The
> second aspect of God's work in his creatures is that he extends
> his hand to help his servants and to punish the wicked. . . . The
> third aspect of the work of God consists in his governance of the
> faithful, living and reigning in them by his Holy Spirit.[12]

Hence, J.I. Packer rightly states that John Calvin's theism
(and Calvinism in general) is to be viewed as "a unified
philosophy of history which sees the whole diversity of
processes and events that take place in God's world as no more,
and no less, than the outworking of his great preordained plan
for his creatures and his church."[13]

Calvin teaches that God is the eternal first cause of all
things. At the same time, men are fully responsible for their
actions (*Institutes* I:17:3; III:23:7). Calvin finds no paradox in
these two teachings. Here again the Reformer is completely in
line with the Westminster Confession of Faith (V:2, 3), which
states:

Although, in relation to the foreknowledge and decree of God, the first cause, all things come to pass immutably, and infallibly; yet, by the same providence, he ordereth them to fall out, according to the nature of second causes, either necessarily, freely, or contingently. . . . God, in his ordinary providence, maketh use of means, yet is free to work without, above, and against them, at his pleasure.

In this schema, the wind, rain, sinful acts of men, miracles, and so forth, are all second causes, used by God to accomplish his sovereign purposes (*Institutes* I:16:5,7). Christianity avers that the eternal decrees of a sovereign, benevolent God govern the course of the universe. Calvin approvingly cites Basil and Augustine in claiming that fortune (luck) and chance are pagan terms, not to be used within Christian circles. When such words are found in Scripture they are to be understood as "seemingly" contingent events as man looks upon them; whereas in actuality the Christian man knows that all things come from God (I:16:8,9).

According to Calvin and the Westminster Assembly,[14] even the sinful acts of men are included in the Triune God's sovereign governing of his universe (as a part of his decretive will), and not by "a bare permission"; he positively wills it (*Institutes* II:4:3; III:23:8). Because God is sovereign, men are not exculpated from their evil deeds. Sin is a violation of the preceptive will of God; thus, God is not to be considered the author of evil (I:17:5; 18:4; II:4:3; III:23:8). According to Calvin, even though all evil in the world is ultimately to be viewed as a result of God's decree, it nevertheless comes from his decree and not his nature (I:17:5; 18:2).

Calvin also maintains that the doctrine of predestination and providence is one which gives the Christian much comfort. Says the Reformer:

Therefore no one will weigh God's providence properly and profitably but him who considers that his business is with his Maker and the Framer of the universe, and with becoming humility submits himself to fear and reverence. . . . All who will compose themselves to this moderation will not murmur against God on account of their adversities in time past, nor lay the blame for their own wickedness upon Him. . . . But rather let them inquire and learn from Scripture what is pleasing to God so that they may strive toward this under the Spirit's guidance. At the same time, being ready to follow God wherever He calls, they will show in very truth that nothing is more profitable than the knowledge of this doctrine (*Institutes* I:17:2,3).

In one of the most magnificent paragraphs in all of the *Institutes* (1536 edition), Calvin, concerning the doctrine of providence, writes:

By this we confess that we have all our trust fixed in God the Father, whom we acknowledge to be Creator of ourselves and of absolutely all things that have been created, which have been established by the Word, His eternal Wisdom (who is the Son), and by His Power (who is the Holy Spirit). And, as He once established, so now He sustains, nourishes, activates, preserves, by His goodness and power, apart from which all things would immediately collapse and fall into nothingness. But when we call Him almighty and creator of all things, we must ponder such omnipotence of His whereby He works all things in all, and such providence whereby He regulates all things—not of the sort those Sophists fancy: empty, insensate, idle. By faith are we to be persuaded that whatever happens to us, happy or sad, prosperous or adverse, whether it pertains to the body or to the soul, comes to us from Him (sin only being excepted, which is to be imputed to our own wickedness); also by His protection we are kept safe, defended, and preserved from any unfriendly force causing us harm. In short, nothing comes forth from Him to us (since we receive all things from His hand) which is not conducive to our welfare, howsoever things may commonly seem at one time prosperous, at another adverse. Indeed all these things are done to us by Him, not through any worth of ours, nor by any merit to which He owes this grace, nor because we can force His beneficence to make any reciprocal payment.

Rather it is through His fatherly kindness and mercy that He has to do with us, the sole cause of which is His goodness. For this reason, we must take care to give thanks for this very great goodness of His, to ponder it with our hearts, proclaim it with our tongue, and to render such praises as we are able. We should so reverence such a Father with grateful piety and burning love, as to devote ourselves wholly to His service, and honor Him in all things. We should also so receive all adverse things with calm and peaceful hearts, as if from His hand, thinking that His providence so also looks after us and our salvation while it is afflicting and oppressing us. Therefore whatever may finally happen, we are never to doubt or lose faith that we have in Him a propitious and benevolent Father, and no less are to await salvation from Him.[15]

CHAPTER FIVE

CALVIN ON MAN

The Westminster Confession of Faith (IV:2) affirms that

> After God had made all other creatures, he created man,
> male and female, with reasonable and immortal souls, endued
> with knowledge, righteousness, and true holiness, after his own
> image, having the law of God written in their hearts, and power
> to fulfill it; and yet under a possibility of transgressing, being left
> to the liberty of their own will, which was subject unto change.
> Beside this law written in their hearts, they received a command
> not to eat of the tree of the knowledge of good and evil; which
> while they kept, they were happy in their communion with God,
> and had dominion over the creatures.

With this statement John Calvin is in agreement. Man is
the crown of all of God's creation. Man "is the noblest and most
remarkable example of His justice, wisdom, and goodness"
(*Institutes* I:15:1). As God's image, man is set apart from all
other creatures (I:15:3).

A key metaphor in Calvin's view of man, says Brian
Gerrish, is "the mirror of God's goodness." Man is to reflect the
image of his maker.[1] For, said the Reformer, whereas the entire
cosmos is to display the glory of God, man, in his entirety (body
and soul), especially mirrors the Creator.[2]

Man as God's Image

According to Calvin, the "proper seat" of the image of God *(imago Dei)* in man is the soul. The soul is immortal; it is the "nobler part"; it is that part of man by which he reasons and spiritually relates to his maker. And yet every part of man, physical and spiritual, is to reflect God's image by "shining forth" for his glory *(Institutes* I:15:2,3,6). Whereas Roman Catholicism makes a distinction between the words "image" and "likeness" in Genesis 1:26, Calvin does not. He views these terms as practically synonymous *(Commentary* on Genesis 1:26).

The Reformed view of man as God's image is that the image of God has two aspects: metaphysical and ethical. Although Calvin does not use these exact terms, this is clearly his view as well *(Institutes* I:15:3).[3] The former has to do with man as a rational, spiritual, immortal being. This part of the image was defaced by the fall, but not altogether eradicated. The fact that the metaphysical image remains basically intact, but marred, is that which allows non-believers to achieve a certain level of excellence in law, medicine, philosophy, and so forth (II:2:4,15).[4]

The ethical image, which is more restricted in nature, consists of true (ethical) knowledge, righteousness, and holiness (Colossians 3:10; Ephesians 4:24). This part of the image was erased at the fall, to the point where fallen man can do nothing that pleases God. Man is now totally depraved. The ethical image can only be renewed in man by the redemptive work of Jesus Christ *(Institutes* I:15:4). This is why Calvin can say that it is in Christ, as touching his human nature, that we see the image of God in man perfected.

Calvin is in agreement with Augustine that prior to the fall Adam (man) possessed freedom of the will *(i.e.,* free moral agency) and the ability to choose good (righteousness). After the fall, however, Adam lost the ability to choose good.

Although he retained his free moral agency, the ethical image was now totally depraved, and Adam's (man's) every desire was (is) to do evil continually (*Commentary* on Genesis 3:1ff; 6:5; *Institutes* I:15:8; II:2:26,27).

Some recent Reformed thinkers maintain that man's dominion over the creatures is part and parcel of the image of God in man, but Calvin does not. The Genevan in no way denies the importance of the dominion mandate of Genesis 1:26-28, but he avers that dominion comes as a bestowment, grounded in the fact that man is God's image. It is not, therefore, to be identified with the image (*Commentary* on Genesis 1:26-28; *Institutes* I:15:4).

The Constitutional Nature of Man

Calvin maintains, along with the vast majority of Reformed scholars, that man has two parts: a physical body and a non-physical spirit or soul (*Commentary* on Genesis 2:7). This, of course, is in distinction to the monistic view of man (*e.g.*, that of G.C. Berkouwer, who claims that the Bible always views man as the "whole man," rather than as two distinct entities which constitute man as "a living soul")[5] and the trichotomistic view of man (*i.e.*, that man consists of three essential elements: body, soul, and spirit).[6] In his *Institutes*, Calvin contends that the Bible, on many occasions, uses the words soul and spirit as synonyms (I:15:2).

There are three major theories regarding the origin of the soul (*i.e.*, the non-physical element of man):

1. pre-existence: the theory that the souls of men existed in a previous state prior to the creation of the world. These souls are infused into every child at conception or birth. This view originated in Plato and has had little favor within the Christian church.

2. traducianism (Latin *tradux*, "branch" or "shoot"): the

theory that the soul along with the body is propagated by the
human parents of the child.

3. creationism: the theory that the body of man is
propagated by the parents, but the soul is an immediate creation
of God. This is Calvin's view. The Reformer maintains that each
and every soul is as much an *ex nihilo* creation as was the
original creation of the universe (*Institutes* I:15:5).

The Imputation of Sin

Calvin maintained that there is a relationship between
Adam's sin and his descendants. Somehow his sin was imputed
to all his natural children. The question is how? There are three
main theories of imputation:

1. Realism: This was Augustine's view. Realists teach that
the whole human race was seminally present in Adam in the
garden of Eden. The Bible considers Adam to be the natural
head of the human race; all men are ontologically joined to him.
Thus, when Adam sinned, his sin was imputed to the entire race
because all were there with Adam, in his loins (Hebrews
7:9,10).

2. Immediate imputation: This is the prevailing theory
among Reformed theologians. Here Adam is considered to be
both the federal and the natural head of all mankind. He
covenantally (*i.e.,* federally) represented the entire race. Thus,
when he sinned, his sin was immediately imputed to all that he
represented. This immediate imputation leaves all men in a
state of judicial guilt (Romans 5:12-19).

But Adam was also the natural head of mankind. All men
were in his loins. The guilt of Adam's sin is viewed as immediately imputed and the polluted nature is inherited by natural
generation.

3. Mediate imputation: Those who adhere to this theory, in
agreement with the realists, teach that the whole human race
was in the loins of Adam in the garden of Eden. But unlike

realism, mediate imputation maintains that Adam's sin was not immediately imputed to all men. Rather, it is mediated to all through natural generation. Men are not guilty because of Adam's sin; they are guilty only because they are born corrupt.

Calvin held to a somewhat modified version of the mediate view. The Reformer concurred that Adam was both the federal and natural head of the whole human race. But, he said, the sin of Adam was not immediately imputed to all; rather, it is now imputed mediately through natural generation (*Institutes* II:1:5-7; *Commentary* on Romans 5:12-19).[7]

As noted, according to Reformed theology in general, and Calvin specifically, the doctrine of original sin teaches that all men, as a result of the fall, are judicially guilty. Adam's sin is imputed to all. But having inherited a polluted nature, all men (including infants) actually and willingly sin (Ephesians 4:17-19). Original sin is one; actual sins are manifold. The fall left man in a state of "total depravity." That is, fallen man is able to do nothing that pleases God (*Institutes* II:1:8-11; 2:26,27; 3:2-5).

Says Calvin, "But let us observe here, that the will of man is in all things opposed to the divine will; for as much as what is crooked differs from what is straight, so much must be the difference between us and God. . . . [A]ll of them [i.e., fallen men] [are] abominable before God. . . . [T]hey are without any spiritual life" (*Commentary* on Romans 8:7,8). Further, he states, "The whole human race perished in the person of Adam. . . . Dullness and ingratitude follow, for our minds, as they have been blinded, do not perceive what is true. And as all our senses have become perverted, we wickedly defraud God of His glory" (*Institutes* II:6:1).

Calvin's reference to man as a "five foot worm," or as one who is unfit even to associate with "worms, lice, fleas, and vermin," speaks to his view of the state of post-fall man. Calvin does not look on fallen man as worthless (no one made in God's image is worthless), but as completely unworthy of any of God's grace (*Institutes* I:5:4).[8]

Man in the Covenant of Grace

Since the fall, man is in desperate need of a savior. That Savior is first revealed to Adam in Genesis 3:15. This is the initiation of the Covenant of Grace. Adam, in Calvin's opinion, is among the elect of God (*Institutes* II:10:7). Regarding this covenant, Calvin writes, "the first promise of salvation was given to Adam. . . . [There] it glowed like a feeble spark. Then, as it was added to, the light grew in fullness, breaking forth increasingly and shedding its radiance more widely. At last—when all the clouds were dispersed—Christ, the Sun of Righteousness, fully illumined the whole earth" (II:10:20).

CHAPTER SIX

CALVIN ON THE COVENANT

John Calvin was a covenant theologian. He did not fully develop the discipline,[1] but he pointed the way for its further refinement and expansion. Peter A. Lillback acknowledges that covenantal thinking existed in the church prior to Calvin, but he is to be considered "the forerunner of Reformed federal [i.e., covenant] theology."[2] Carl Bogue agrees when he writes that although covenant theology is not the sole "organizing principle" in the Reformer's theology, "the essentials are definitely present."[3]

M.E. Osterhaven claims that development in Calvin's covenant theology is apparent in his writings. In the 1536 edition of the *Institutes* there were only a few uses of the term covenant, but in the later editions of his major work, as well as in his numerous commentaries and sermon series, the usage greatly increases.[4] Undoubtedly, this development in the covenant theology of John Calvin, and other sixteenth century scholars, led to greater development in the theology of the Puritan divines.[5]

Perry Miller (and others), on the other hand, disagrees. He categorically denies that Calvin was a covenant theologian at all. He maintains that covenant theology was a later Puritan development, for the purpose of moving away from the high predestinarian concept of Calvinism. As John Gerstner points out, this is a misunderstanding of John Calvin as well as the

Puritans. Calvin, as the forerunner, and the later Puritans, all viewed the covenants as conditional, that is, God is absolutely sovereign and man is responsible to him.[6]

Interestingly, this was also Martin Luther's (and Lutheranism's) problem with covenant theology. The German Reformer saw the covenant as a *quid pro quo*—man's faith and obedience earn salvation. Again, this is a serious misunderstanding of what covenant theology teaches.[7] (A study of the Greek word *diatheke* [covenant], found in Scripture, would seem to have solved this problem for Luther. A *diatheke* is a covenant agreement between two parties where one party as sovereign establishes conditions for the covenant, etc. The second party is obligated to obey under the grace of the sovereign. All is of grace in a *diatheke* form of covenant. If the covenant were to have existed between two equal parties, where obedience merited favor, then *suntheke*, not *diatheke*, would have been the word used.)[8]

As noted, Calvin held that all biblical covenants are conditional; they are two-sided. That is, God gives commands as well as promises. The latter are pledged by the sovereign God; the former are to be obeyed by his vassals. Covenant breakers will be cut off from God's covenant people, the church, whereas covenant keepers will receive divine blessings (*Commentary* on Genesis 17:19). At the same time, we must recognize that while the covenants are conditional even to the elect, God is the one who supplies their need so that they are able to keep the covenant (*Sermons* on Deuteronomy 7:11-15; 27:11-15).

In his *Sermons* on Deuteronomy (26:16-19), Calvin taught that the only way that man is able to have any relationship with God is that God has deigned to enter into covenant with his creatures. Thus, Calvin's position would be similar to that of the Westminster Confession of Faith (VII:1):

> The distance between God and the creature is so great, that although reasonable creatures do owe obedience unto Him as their Creator, yet they could never have any fruition of Him as

their blessedness and reward, but by some voluntary condescension on God's part, which He hath been pleased to express by way of covenant.

Calvin views the covenant as essential to a proper understanding of the unity of Scripture, God's work in salvation, Christian living, the reformation of the church, and the sacraments. In fact, he strongly insists that the concept of covenant is that which makes the people of God one: both Old and New Testaments (*Institutes* II:10,11).

Calvin does recognize the federal headship of Adam in God's initial covenant agreement (*Commentary* on Romans 5:12; 1 Corinthians 15:45), but he nowhere refers to it as a "covenant of works." He does, on the other hand, maintain that Genesis 3:15 is the beginning of the covenant of grace,[9] a covenant which remains and progresses throughout redemptive history, until it is fulfilled in the coming of Christ. He writes:

> [T]he first promise of salvation was given to Adam. . . . [T]here it glowed like a feeble spark. Then, as it was added to, the light grew in fullness, breaking forth increasingly and shedding its radiance more widely. At last—when all the clouds were dispersed—Christ, the Sun of Righteousness, fully illumined the whole earth (*Institutes* II:10:20).

The Reformer notes the progressive aspect of this one covenant of grace as follows. Covenant promises, says Calvin, were given to both Adam and Noah, along with covenant signs (*Institutes* IV:14:6,18). But the covenant of grace really came into its own with Abraham and his seed (III:21:7; *Commentary* on Genesis 12:3; 17:1ff.). Once given to Abraham, this covenant continues to flow through redemptive history, reaching its Old Testament zenith in David, as a type of Christ (*Commentary* on Psalm 89:3ff.). And then, having come into its fullest measure with the advent of Christ himself, the covenant remains as valid for us today as it was to Israel. Calvin writes: "It is most evident that the covenant which the Lord once made with Abraham is no less in force today for Christians than it was of old for the Jewish people" (*Institutes* IV:16:6).

In Calvin's thought, there are not two covenants—the Old and the New—in some radical sense; rather, these two are really "one and the same" covenant (*Institutes* II:10:2).[10] It is the covenant of grace which gives unity to the people of God: Old and New Testaments; they are all saved by grace. Says Calvin:

> [T]he Old Testament was established upon the free mercy of God, and was confirmed by Christ's intercession. For the gospel preaching, too, declares nothing else than that sinners are justified apart from their own merit by God's fatherly kindness; and the whole of it is summed up in Christ. Who, then, dares to separate the Jews from Christ, since, with them . . . was made the covenant of the gospel, the sole foundation of which is Christ? Who dares to estrange from the gift of free salvation those to whom we hear the doctrine of the righteousness of faith imparted? (II:10:4).

Thus, Calvin can write that all of the Old Testament saints, from Adam onward, belonged to the New Covenant in that they embraced Christ, the promised Messiah (*Institutes* II:11:10). The covenant promise of God to all of his covenant children (Old and New Testaments) is the same: He is their God, and they are his people. In this way the God of Scripture has covenanted with them all (II:10:8). The perpetuity of the covenant, notes the Reformer, is guaranteed in Deuteronomy 5:2ff. (*Sermons* on Deuteronomy 4:44-5:3).

This does not mean, however, that for Calvin there is no difference between the two dispensations of the one covenant of grace. The Old Testament promises what the New delivers in Christ. The New Covenant is one of greater realization; it is one of greater power in the Holy Spirit; and, in this respect, it is superior.[11] Like the Westminster divines, John Calvin maintained that the Old Testament church was the "church under age" (*Commentary* on Hebrews 8:10).[12]

According to Calvin, the covenant is also that which gives

unity to the Word of God and the sacraments. As to the former, the Geneva Reformer does not radically separate the Old and New Testaments, the law and the gospel. He recognizes that the Bible is one covenant book, which belongs to the people of God throughout all ages. The same Holy Spirit inspired writers of the Old and New Testaments; both are the eternal unchanging Word of God (*Commentary* on Psalm 119:89; Isaiah 40:8).

In fact, writes Calvin, the immutable law of God is included in the covenant of grace (*Institutes* II:7:2). Wilhelm Niesel says that Calvin "praised the glory of the law because he recognized it to be the covenantal law of the gracious and faithful God, and imparted by Him to His church."[13] In one of his most brilliant works of exegesis, Calvin shows that the same Holy Spirit is necessary in both Testaments for the illumination of God's Word to non-believers; he is the one who gives life to the law (*Commentary* on 2 Corinthians 3:1-16).

Moreover, in his *Commentary* on Matthew 5:17, Calvin states:

> God had, indeed, promised a New Covenant at the coming of Christ; but had, at the same time, showed that it would not be different from the first, but that, on the contrary, its design was, to give a perpetual sanction to the covenant, which He had made from the beginning with His people. "I will write my law," (says He) "in their hearts, and I will remember their iniquities no more" (Jeremiah 31:33,34). By these words He is so far from departing from the former covenant, that on the contrary, He declares, that it will be confirmed and ratified, when it shall be succeeded by the New. This is also the meaning of Christ's words when He says that He came to fulfill the law: for He actually fulfilled it by quickening with His Spirit the dead letter and then exhibiting, in reality, what had hitherto appeared only in figures.

John Calvin would also be in full agreement with the Westminster divines regarding covenant theology and the sacraments. That is, both Baptism and the Lord's Supper are to be considered as signs and seals of the covenant of grace

(*Institutes* IV:14:1-6).[14] Further, Calvin is in full accord with Westminster that "The sacraments of the Old Testament, in regard of the spiritual things thereby signified and exhibited, were, for substance, the same with those of the New."[15] Christ, says the Reformer, was promised in the "ancient sacraments" (*Institutes* IV:14:20).

Calvin specifically says this in his *Commentary* on 1 Corinthians 10:1-13. There he comments that "the ancient sacraments of the law had the same virtue as ours have at this day. . . . [T]he reality of the sacraments was presented to the people of God no less than to us." When the Jews ate the Old Testament covenant feast they partook of Christ, for

> even though His flesh did not as yet exist, it was nevertheless, food for them. . . . The promises given to them shadowed forth the gospel in such a way, that they had it included in them. Their sacraments served to prefigure ours in such a way that they were nevertheless, even for that period, true sacraments, having a present efficacy.

At the same time that the substance of the sacraments was the same as ours, yet we have a fuller revelation and feasting: "Christ is now presented to us more fully."

In John Calvin's covenant theology, the whole of biblical revelation, salvation, and corporate solidarity among all of God's people hold together. Indeed, the Genevan Reformer might not have developed the concept of covenant as fully as did his successors. But he certainly laid the groundwork necessary for that later development.

CHAPTER SEVEN

CALVIN ON CHRIST

John Calvin was in agreement with his contemporary Martin Luther, the great German Reformer, who once wrote:

> The history of the church universal has confirmed in me the conviction that those who have had and maintained the central article in its integrity, that of Jesus Christ, have remained safely intrenched in their Christian faith. . . . [H]e who steadfastly holds to the doctrine that Jesus Christ is true God and true man, who died and rose again for us, will acquiesce in and heartily assent to all the other articles of the Christian faith.[1]

Theologians normally divide the study of Christology (the doctrine of Jesus Christ) into two parts, his person and his work. Calvin does this as well. These two doctrinal studies are inseparable, for we can never understand the work of the mediator without first understanding his person. That is why Calvin, in his *Institutes,* begins with the latter (II:12-14) and concludes with the former (II:15-17).[2]

The Person of Christ

The Council of Chalcedon (A.D. 451) declared that Jesus Christ is:

> Truly God and truly man, of a reasonable soul and body; consubstantial with the Father according to the Godhead, and consubstantial with us according to his manhood; in all things like unto us without sin; begotten before all ages of the Father according to the Godhead, and in these latter days, for us and for our salvation, born of the Virgin Mary, the Mother of God, according to the manhood; one and the same Christ, Son, Lord, Only-begotten, to be acknowledged in two natures inconfusedly, unchangeably, indivisibly, inseparably; the distinction of natures being by no means taken away by the union, but rather the property of each nature being preserved, and concurring in one Person and one Subsistence, not parted or divided into two persons, but one and the same Son, Only-begotten, God, the Word, the Lord Jesus Christ.

As G.C. Berkouwer points out, through the centuries of time the church has not improved on this creedal statement. Calvin does not attempt to; he merely expands upon the truths expressed in the Chalcedonian formula.[3]

The Divine Nature

As we have seen in chapter 4, the Reformer maintained that Jesus Christ, the eternal second person of the triune Godhead, is fully divine (*Institutes* I:13:7-13). There we noted that in his *Commentaries* on Romans 9:5, Titus 2:13, Hebrews 1:8, and 1 John 5:20, Calvin avers that Christ is God *(auto theos)* in his own right.

According to Calvin, Christ is the "eternal and essential Word of the Father" (*Institutes* I:13:7). He is of one essence with the Father (*Commentary* on Philippians 2:6). The same divine Son of God, albeit pre-incarnate, appeared to the patriarchs under the Old Testament economy and has now appeared, incarnate, to us under the New (I:13:10). In the incarnation, God has manifested himself to his people "fully," "perfectly," and "wholly" (*Commentary* on Colossians 2:9).

Further, at the incarnation, the Lord Jesus laid aside none of his divine attributes (*Commentary* on John 1:14). The divine nature, by definition, can never change (*i.e.,* God is immutable). Writes Calvin, "The Son of God descended from heaven in such a way that, without leaving heaven, He willed to be borne in the virgin's womb, to go about the earth, and to hang upon the cross; yet, He continuously filled the world even as He had done from the beginning" (*Institutes* II:13:4).[4] The *Kenosis* doctrine of modernist theologians cannot be traced to Calvin.

The Human Nature *fram belaw*

Calvin, with Chalcedon, also holds to the fact that Jesus Christ was fully human as well as fully divine (*Institutes* II:13:1-4). He cites numerous Scripture passages to prove his point: Matthew 1:1; Romans 1:3, 9:5; Galatians 4:4; Hebrews 2:14,16, 4:15; Philippians 2:5-8; 1 Peter 3:18 (II:13:1,2). The virgin birth is further biblical proof of the human nature of Jesus (II:13:3). Even the name "Son of Man" speaks to his humanity (II:13:2). (Calvin does not deny that the name "Son of Man" has divine implications as well.)

When Jesus took upon himself a human nature, he became "a real man composed of body and soul" (*Institutes* II:13:2). That is, he was (and still is) human in the full sense of the word. During his earthly ministry, Christ was subject to "hunger, thirst, cold, and other infirmities of our nature" (*Institutes* II:13:1). Further, "he chose not only to grow in body but to make progress in mind" (*Commentary* on Luke 2:40). The thing, of course, which distinguishes Christ's humanity from ours is that he is "free from all fault and corruption," *i.e.,* sinless (II:13:4).

According to Calvin, it is absolutely essential that Jesus Christ be both God and man. Only then, as mediator, could he bridge the gap between the holy God and sinful man. As man, Christ tasted death in behalf of his people; as God he overcame it. It is the divine nature which gives Christ's sacrifice infinite value (*Institutes* II:12:1-3; *Commentary* on Hebrews 2:14). If Christ is not both fully God and fully man, then salvation is not possible (*Commentary* on Matthew 22:42; Hebrews 5:1). Thus, as a consequence of God's decree to save the elect, the incarnation was "absolutely necessary." There was no other way (*Institutes* II:12:1).

The Unity of the Person

Theologians call the union of the divine and human natures of Jesus Christ in one person "the hypostatic union." As expressed in the Chalcedonian formula, this doctrine maintains that the eternal Son of God took upon himself an impersonal human nature: body and soul. He did not become or adopt a human person; he assumed a human nature. The human nature did not become an independent personality. Rather, it became personal in the person of the eternal Son. Therefore, although the Lord has two distinct natures, he is only one person. With this definition of the unity of the person, John Calvin is in agreement (*Institutes* II:14:1-8). In fact, he states that the best human analogy that we can use to explain this union is that of the mysterious union of the human spirit and body which composes man (II:14:1).

Further, the two natures of Christ are never to be confused (*i.e.*, mixed in any fashion) or separated (*Institutes* II:14:2). Yet they must remain distinct. Says Calvin, "The unity of the person does not hinder the two natures from remaining distinct, so that his divinity retains all that is peculiar to itself, and his humanity holds separately whatever belongs to it" (*Commentary* on John 1:14). As noted earlier, in his *Institutes* (II:13:4), the Reformer maintains that at one and the same time, the one person of Jesus Christ, as touching his human nature, could be "borne in the virgin's womb . . . go about the earth . . . hang on the cross," and yet, as touching his divine nature, "He continuously filled the world even as He had done from the beginning."

One of the effects of the hypostatic union is that of the communication of attributes. This means that whatever can be attributed to either the divine or to the human nature of Christ is attributed to the one person. For example, the Bible speaks of the person of Jesus Christ sleeping in the back of a boat (Mark 4:38), whereas we know that God does not sleep (Psalm 121:4). Likewise, Acts 20:28 refers to the blood of God which is shed on the cross; but God is pure Spirit (John 4:24) and does not have blood (Luke 24:39). In each of these cases that which is said about Christ is attributed to his person.

Concerning this doctrine, Calvin writes that the Scriptures,

> sometimes attribute to Him [Christ] what must be referred solely to His humanity, sometimes what belongs uniquely to His divinity; and sometimes what embraces both natures but fits neither alone. And they so earnestly express this union of the two natures that is in Christ as sometimes to interchange them. This figure of speech is called by the ancient writers the communication of properties [*i.e.*, attributes] (*Institutes* II:14:1).

Throughout the history of the church numerous heresies have arisen regarding the person of Christ. Millard Erickson notes that there are basically six such heresies, all of which appeared in some fashion within the first four centuries after Christ. He observes: "They [the heresies] either deny the genuineness (Ebionism) or the completeness (Arianism) of Jesus' deity, deny the genuineness (Docetism) or the completeness (Apollinarianism) of his humanity, divide the person (Nestorianism), or confuse his natures (Eutychianism). All departures from the orthodox doctrine of the person of Christ are simply variations of one of these heresies."[5] John Calvin, with typical incisiveness, skillfully avoided all.

When dealing with the subject of the person of Christ, it is also customary for Reformed theologians to speak of the "states of Christ." This has to do with the mediator's position under the law of God. Christ, as the divine lawgiver (James 4:12), took upon himself a human nature and came under the law (Galatians 4:4). That is, during the time of his humiliation, Christ was a servant under the law. In his state of exaltation, this is no longer the case. This doctrine is well expressed in the Westminster Shorter Catechism (Q. 27, 28):

> Christ's humiliation consisted in his being born, and that in a low condition, made under the law, undergoing the miseries of this life, the wrath of God, and the cursed death of the cross; in being buried, and continuing under the power of death for a time. . . . Christ's exaltation consisteth in his rising again from the dead on the third day, in ascending up into heaven, in sitting at the right hand of God the Father, and in coming to judge the world at the last day.

As this doctrine was basically a seventeenth century development, Calvin did not discuss the topic separately. Nevertheless, his teaching on the subject is clearly manifest in his various writings. For example, in his 1536 edition of the *Institutes,* and in his *Catechism of the Church of Geneva,* Calvin discourses on the doctrine of Christ as contained in the Apostles Creed. There we find a thorough teaching on the states of Christ, albeit not under that title, which fully agrees with Westminster (see also *Institutes* II:16:1-19).

The Work of Christ

When Reformed theologians study the work of Jesus Christ, they normally do so under the rubric of his three offices: prophet, priest, and king. Interestingly, although others (*e.g.,* Augustine and Aquinas) before him had spoken of Christ's ministry in this three-fold fashion, it was John Calvin who fully developed this approach (*Institutes* II:15:1-6).

The New Testament title Christ *(christos),* which is the equivalent of the Old Testament Messiah *(mashiach),* means "anointed one." In the Old Covenant era, prophets (1 Kings 19:16), priests (Exodus 29:7; Psalm 133:2), and kings (1 Samuel 10:1; 16:13), were anointed to carry out their God-given functions. The same is true of Jesus Christ. In Matthew 3:16, 17, we read that he was anointed by the Holy Spirit to carry out his three-fold office (*Commentary* on Matthew 3:16, 17; *Institutes* II:15:1).

As prophet, Christ executes his office "in revealing to us, by his Word and Spirit, the will of God for our salvation."[6] This office, says Calvin, was carried out under the Old Covenant era by means of his prophets, through whom he was speaking (*Commentary* on 1 Peter 1:10-12). In the New Covenant, Christ came as the great prophet himself to be our teacher. But after his ascension, he continued his prophetic ministry through the apostles, and now in the church through gospel ministers who truly preach his Word (*Institutes* II:15:1,2). God, says Calvin, cannot be known except "through Christ" (*Commentary* on 1 Peter 1:21).

As priest, Jesus Christ executes his office "in His once offering up of Himself as a sacrifice to satisfy divine justice, and reconcile us to God; and in making continual intercession for us"[7] (*Institutes* II:15:6). According to Calvin, the purpose of Christ's incarnation was the redemption of the elect (II:12:4). (Calvin's supralapsarianism is evident here: the purpose of creation was to glorify God through the redemption of the church [II:12:5].)

The Lord Jesus lived a sinless life in active obedience to the will of God, thus fulfilling the covenant of works (Calvin does not use the term "covenant of works") on behalf of the elect (*Commentary* on Romans 5:17-19; *Institutes* II:13:4; 16:5). Then he went to the cross, as a one-time sacrifice, to atone for their sins, in what is called his passive obedience (II:15:6). (The entirety of Christ's sufferings during his earthly ministry is referred to as his passive obedience.)[8]

In his *Commentary* on Isaiah 53:5, Calvin teaches that

during his entire earthly life, Christ was bearing away the sins of the elect. In the words of Robert Peterson:

> Calvin's conception of the saving work of Christ was a broad one. Although he saw the cross as the heart of the atonement, he did not confine the work of Christ to the cross. The incarnation, the life of Christ, the crucifixion, the descent, the resurrection, the ascension, and the second coming of Christ are all redemptive. They are components of one grand redemptive plan, the center of which is the cross.[9]

At Calvary, double imputation occurred. Christ's righteousness was imputed to the elect, while at the same time, their sins were imputed to him. Thus, the sins of God's people, through the priestly work of Christ, are gone; they are remembered no more (*Institutes* II:16:5,6; *Commentary* on 2 Corinthians 5:21). Hence, Calvin can say that it is on the cross that the glory of God shines most brightly (*Commentary* on John 13:31).

It was on the cross, says the Reformer, that Christ was forsaken by the Father. Here he suffered the torments of hell on behalf of the elect. This, according to Calvin, is where Christ "descended into hell," as per the Apostles Creed (*Institutes* II:16:10). In fact, the Genevan preferred to restructure the lines of the Creed as follows: "suffered under Pontius Pilate, was crucified, descended into hell, dead, and buried"; this he believed would better reflect the biblical teaching that the God-man received the punishment of hell while he was on the cross.[10]

Christ's priestly work, however, did not cease at the cross. As the ascended Lord of glory, he sits at the Father's right hand where he continually intercedes on behalf of the elect (*Institutes* II:15:6). In his *Commentary* on Hebrews 7:25, Calvin states that the ascended Christ is now "performing his office as priest; for it belongs to a priest to intercede for the people, that they may obtain favor with God. This is what Christ is ever doing . . . ."

The fact that Christ, as intercessor, is now at the Father's right hand guarantees that the prayers of the saints will be heard and answered. To pray in his name is to have "the blood of Christ . . . always distilling before the presence of the Father" (*Commentary* on Hebrews 10:19). In other words, just as the process of distillation purifies a liquid and brings it down to its basic essence, so also the intercessory work of Christ purifies the prayers of all those he bought through his death.[11]

As king, Christ executes his office "in subduing us to Himself, in ruling and defending us, and in restraining and conquering all His and our enemies"[12] (*Institutes* II:15:3-5). Calvin here stresses the spiritual nature of Christ's mediatorial kingship. As eternal deity, Christ has always been king. But in the fullness of time, he came in the flesh to rule over his church. In this capacity, Christ subdues us to himself, rules over and defends us, and restrains and conquers all of our enemies. Yet, at the same time, Christ is universal king. He reigns over this universe as king of kings and lord of lords. Progressively, he is subduing his enemies under his feet in accordance with his will (II:14:3-5).

The Atonement

As noted above, there is a sense in which we can say that Calvin held that the atonement was the purpose of the incarnation. Says the Reformer, "the only end which the Scripture uniformly assigns for the Son of God voluntarily assuming our nature, and even receiving it as a command from the Father, is, that He might propitiate the Father to us by becoming a victim" (*Institutes* II:12:4). This, of course, is a part of the Son's priestly ministry.

Calvin draws his theology on the atonement, not only from the New Testament revelation, but also from the Old. Robert Paul is correct when he states that not nearly enough attention has been given to the Reformer's teachings on the Old Covenant sacrificial system and the light they shed upon the

entirety of the atoning work of Christ.[13]
    For example, Calvin writes:

> [F]or what is more vain or absurd than for men to offer a loathsome stench from the fat of cattle in order to reconcile themselves to God? Or to have recourse to the sprinkling of water and blood to cleanse away filth? In short, the whole cultus of the law, taken literally and not as shadows and figures corresponding to the truth, will be utterly ridiculous (*Institutes* II:7:1).

In other words, Calvin is saying that no true Israelite would have considered his salvation to be rooted in the blood of bulls and goats, but in the Christ represented in those offerings. Says the Genevan, "from the beginning of the world Christ was held forth to all the elect as the object of their faith and confidence" (*Institutes* II:6:4).

A review of Calvin's writings, particularly in the "second part" of his commentary on the Apostles Creed found in the 1536 edition of the *Institutes* and the final (1559) edition of the *Institutes* (II:12,15-17), reveals the following regarding his view of the atonement:[14]

1. It was sufficient to save all men, but it was only efficient to save the elect.[15] It was unlimited in power, but limited (or particular) in extent.

2. It was a propitiatory sacrifice (*Commentary* on Matthew 26:3; 1 John 2:1,2). The atonement took away the sins of the elect, and appeased the wrath of God, thus satisfying his justice. Anselm (c. 1033-1109) had earlier endorsed this view of the atonement, which is known as the Satisfaction Theory. (Calvin here would be in radical disagreement with those [*e.g.*, C.H. Dodd] who deny the propitiatory aspect of Christ's atonement.)[16]

3. It was a penal sacrifice, in that Christ suffered the penalty for the sins of his people (*Commentary* on Luke 22:37; 2 Corinthians 5:21).

4. It was a substitutionary sacrifice (*Commentary* on Isaiah 53:10). Jesus Christ suffered vicariously on behalf of his sheep.

He was not a third party. As God, he was the offended party; and sin could only be forgiven because God, in Christ, willingly took the penalty due the elect.

5. It was a one-time sacrifice in which Christ accomplished redemption on behalf of the elect (*Institutes* II:17:1-5; *Commentary* on Hebrews 9:26).

6. It was a ransom. Guilty sinners owed a sin debt to God (not Satan). Christ paid the ransom to the Father on their behalf, thus redeeming them and bringing about reconciliation (*Commentary* on Colossians 1:21; *Institutes* III:2:2).

7. It was rooted in the covenant which God had established with his elect (*Commentary* on Hebrews 9:15-18).

8. It has as its starting point God's free love in Christ (*Commentary* on John 3:16; Hebrews 2:9).[17]

9. It was an atonement wherein Christ conquered the four main enemies of the Christian faith: Satan, death, sin, and the world. He destroyed the enemies of God's people and emerged as victor.[18]

CHAPTER EIGHT

CALVIN ON SALVATION

Although the work of salvation involves all three members of the Godhead, the Holy Spirit is the one who applies this grace to the elect. The salvation of the elect from start to finish is due to their relationship with Christ; that is, their being in union with him. The elect are in union with their Savior in that he is their federal head. He represents them just as Adam represented all men in the garden of Eden. This union with Christ is brought about by the work of the Spirit. He, says Calvin, "is the bond by which Christ effectually unites us to Himself" (*Institutes* III:1:1). (In his *Institutes* [II:17:2; III:24:5], Calvin correctly states that the only way that God the Father can love the elect is in Christ; apart from him, they are filthy in sin and hated by God.)

In his *Commentary* on Ephesians 1 and 2, Calvin expounds on the richness of being in union with Christ: blessed in Christ, chosen in him, having been predestinated unto adoption by Jesus Christ, having redemption through his blood, being sealed by the Spirit in him, spiritually resurrected in Christ, created in him unto good works, and so forth.

In one section of the *Institutes* (II:16:19), the Reformer speaks eloquently on the magnificence of the doctrine of the union of Christ and his people:

> We see that our whole salvation and all its parts are

comprehended in Christ (Acts 4:12). We should therefore take care not to derive the least portion of it from anywhere else. If we seek salvation, we are taught by the very name of Jesus that it is "of Him" (1 Corinthians 1:30). If we seek any other gifts of the Spirit, they will be found in His anointing. If we seek strength, it lies in His dominion; if purity, in His conception; if gentleness, it appears in His birth. For by His birth He was made like us in all respects (Hebrews 2:17) that He might learn to feel our pain (cf. Hebrews 5:2). If we seek redemption, it lies in His passion; if acquittal, in His condemnation; if remission of the curse, in His cross (Gal. 3:13); if satisfaction, in His sacrifice; if purification, in His blood; if reconciliation, in His descent into hell; if mortification of the flesh, in His tomb; if newness of life, in His resurrection; if immortality, in the same; if inheritance of the heavenly Kingdom, in His entrance into heaven; if protection, if security, if abundant supply of all blessings, in His Kingdom; if untroubled expectation of judgment, in the power given to Him to judge. In short, since rich store of every kind of good abounds in Him, let us drink our fill from this fountain, and from no other. Some men, not content with Him alone, are borne hither and thither from one hope to another; even if they concern themselves chiefly with Him, they nevertheless stray from the right way in turning some part of their thinking in another direction. Yet such distrust cannot creep in where men have once for all truly known the abundance of His blessings.

Salvation, then, is not to be considered as many distinct acts of redemption. Rather it is to be viewed as distinct aspects of a single act, temporally worked out in an orderly fashion, with the doctrine of the believer's union with Christ underlying them and binding them together.

The Order of Salvation

Soteriology (from the Greek *soter,* savior) is the study of the work of redemption done by Christ, as it is applied in the hearts and lives of the elect. There is a logical order, referred to as the *ordo salutis* (order of salvation), in which this work is carried out.[1] That is, salvation is not a one step event. One is not converted and immediately glorified. Passages such as John 1:12,13, Romans 8:28-30, and Ephesians 1:3-14 and 2:8-10, teach us that there is a process involved; to quote Calvin, it is a "graduating process." But even as we study the process, as given to us by the Genevan Reformer, we must keep in mind that some of the parts of the *ordo salutis* may be synchronous; and the parts "can by no means be separated" (*Commentary* on Romans 8:30).

According to Calvin and Reformed theology in general, the order of the application of redemption occurs as follows:

1. The external or universal call is that "general call, by which God invites all equally to Himself through the outward preaching of the Word—even those to whom He holds it out as a savor of death . . . and as the occasion for severer condemnation" (*Institutes* III:24:8).

When Calvin speaks of the universal call of the gospel, he does not mean to say that God "earnestly desires" that all who hear the invitation will be saved. This would be little more than incipient Arminianism. God only desires the salvation of the elect; they are the ones to whom the call becomes effectual. The same God who wills to save the elect also wills to condemn the reprobate (*Institutes* III:24:1,2,8).

2. The universal call of the gospel becomes effectual when the Spirit applies it to the heart of the elect (*Institutes* III:24:8). Divine election takes place before creation, but effectual calling occurs in history (*Commentary* on Ephesians 1:4-6; Matthew 11:25-30). Regarding the relationship between the two, Calvin would have us ask, Why do many hear the gospel preached and only some respond? Certainly it is not due to the inherent goodness of the latter! The answer is simply that God has chosen some to respond and others not to (*Commentary* on Psalm 65:4; *Institutes* III:21:1; 24:12).

This call is irresistible; the person called of God will be

saved (*Commentary* on Romans 8:30). Calvin writes, "Grace is by no means offered by God only to be rejected or accepted as it may seem good to one; it is the same grace alone which inclines our heart to follow its movement, and produces in it the choice as much as the will" (*Institutes* II:3:13).

3. Although effectual calling and regeneration stand in the closest possible relationship, there is a distinction. Regeneration is a work of the Holy Spirit, a result of his effectual call, by which He prepares the heart of the individual to respond to the call of God. At this point, the sinner is "born again" by God (*Commentary* on John 3:3-8). "It is therefore the Spirit of God who regenerates us, and makes us new creatures . . . [and] the Spirit is bestowed on none but those who are the members of Christ" (*Commentary* on Titus 3:5,6). One of the major differences between Calvinists and Arminians is found at this point. Calvinists teach that regeneration precedes faith; Arminians claim that faith precedes regeneration.

Care, however, must be taken here in reading Calvin, because in the *Institutes* (III:3:1-9) he claims that faith precedes regeneration and repentance. The Reformer uses the word "regeneration," as well as "repentance," not so much as the new birth, which is sovereignly bestowed upon God's elect, but as the new life in general. The Puritans, and Reformed theology in general, have used the word regeneration as it is used in this book.

4. Conversion is that gracious act of God by which he causes regenerated persons to respond to the effectual call. It consists of two parts: repentance and faith. These two go hand in hand; they cannot be separated (*Commentary* on Mark 1:14,15).

Repentance unto life "is a saving grace, whereby a sinner, out of a true sense of his sin, and apprehension of the mercy of God in Christ, doth with grief and hatred of sin, turn from it unto God, with full purpose of, and endeavour after, new obedience."[2] Saving faith in Jesus Christ "is a saving grace, whereby we receive and rest upon him alone for salvation, as he is offered to us in the gospel."[3]

Simply stated, repentance is a turning from sin; faith is a turning to Christ. Biblical repentance (Greek: *metanoia*), says Calvin, involves a change of mind (this is the meaning of *metanoia) (Institutes* III:3:5). The repentant sinner changes his whole attitude toward sin; he is induced "by the fear of God" to radically deal with sin in his life (III:7:4). And having turned away from sin, the believer turns his whole life about to serve the Lord with a godly fear (III:3:6,7).

Saving faith, which is inseparably joined with biblical repentance, is "A firm and certain knowledge of God's benevolence toward us, founded upon the truth of the freely-given promise in Christ, both revealed to our minds and sealed upon our hearts through the Holy Spirit" (*Institutes* III:2:7).

To Calvin, then, saving faith and the Word of God are inextricably bound together. Such faith rests upon the Word, and it is applied by means of the Holy Spirit (*Institutes* III:2:6,33). This faith will grow during the process of sanctification, as the believer studies the Word of God and meditates upon it. The more he gives himself to this discipline, the clearer his understanding will become and the greater his faith will grow (I:14:21; *Commentary* on Mark 8:22-26; Ephesians 3:18).

According to the Reformer, saving faith involves three elements: knowledge *(notitia),* assent *(assensus),* and trust *(fiducia).* It is not enough for one to know the truth about Jesus Christ *(notitia);* nor is it sufficient to merely assent to the gospel message *(assensus),* as essential as these are. Saving faith is that which also wholeheartedly acquiesces to the Christ revealed in Scripture. Biblical conversion involves a whole-souled commitment (*Institutes* III:2:1-13,36).

5. According to the Westminster Assembly, "justification is an act of God's free grace, wherein he pardoneth all our sins, and accepteth us as righteous in his sight, only for the righteousness of Christ imputed to us, and received by faith

alone."[4] Calvin agrees (*Institutes* III:11:1-23).

The doctrine of justification by faith alone was the heart of the Reformation. It was, according to Martin Luther, "the article by which the church stands or falls"; to Calvin, it was "the hinge of the Reformation," "the principal article of the Christian religion," "the principle of the whole doctrine of salvation and the foundation of all religion." The Protestant church stood upon this major tenet of Christianity, whereas Roman Catholicism at the Council of Trent (1546-63) fell away by rejecting it.[5]

It is clear, however, that when the Reformers spoke of this doctrine of justification "by faith alone," what they meant was "by Christ alone"; that is, the ground of justification is Christ's vicarious righteousness and sacrifice. Faith is in no way to be considered as meritorious (*Institutes* III:11:23). Faith, of course, means trusting in Christ who alone justifies. Salvation is by God's grace *(sola gratia)* through faith *(sola fide)*. Faith is the instrument by which one is saved, not the cause of one's salvation.

Calvin writes, "Our justification rests upon God's mercy alone and Christ's merit, and faith, when it lays hold of justification, is said to justify . . . . [W]e say that faith justifies, not because it merits righteousness for us by its own worth, but because it is an instrument whereby we obtain free the righteousness of Christ" (*Institutes* III:18:8).

Further, this justification is forensic; it is a legal act. Justification is imputed, not infused (*i.e.,* man is not made righteous in justification, as in Roman Catholicism). It is an alien righteousness that justifies us (*Commentary* on 2 Corinthians 5:21). In his 1536 edition of the *Institutes,* Calvin writes:

> [T]he righteousness of faith is Christ's righteousness, not our own, that it is in Him and not in us, but that it becomes ours by imputation. . . . thus we are not really righteous, except by imputation; and we are unrighteous but held to be righteous by imputation, in so far as we possess the righteousness of Christ by faith.[6]

Although, according to John Calvin and the Reformers, justification is by faith alone, faith is not alone. That is, true saving faith will yield good works. Justifying faith is not faith plus works (as per Rome); neither is it faith minus (*i.e.*, without necessary) works (as in Antinomianism); it is a faith that works. The works, however, are not works of merit, but of necessity. Says Calvin, and Reformational theology, "justification is by faith alone inseparably connected with works"[7] (*Institutes* III:11:13-23). Calvin writes:

> [W]e must not put any trust in works, or glory in any esteem of them. The agreement lies in this: that the saints, when it is a question of the founding and establishing of their own salvation, without regard for works turn their eyes solely to God's goodness. Not only do they betake themselves to it before all things as to the beginning of blessedness but they repose in it as in the fulfillment of this. A conscience so founded, erected, and established is established also in the consideration of works, so far, that is, as these are testimonies of God dwelling and ruling in us. Inasmuch, therefore, as this reliance upon works has no place unless you first cast the whole confidence of your mind upon God's mercy, it ought not to seem contrary to that upon which it depends. Therefore, when we rule out reliance upon works, we mean only this: that the Christian mind may not be turned back to the merit of works as to a help toward salvation but should rely wholly on the free promise of righteousness. But we do not forbid him from undergirding and strengthening this faith by signs of the divine benevolence toward him. For if, when all the gifts God has bestowed upon us are called to mind, they are like rays of the divine countenance by which we are illumined to contemplate that supreme light of goodness; much more is this true of the grace of good works, which shows that the Spirit of adoption has been given to us (*Institutes* III:14:18).

(6) Adoption is a judicial act of God by which he brings the justified sinner into a filial relationship with himself. Adopted sons and daughters participate in all the inheritance rights of God's elect (*Commentary* on Hebrews 2:5). Such privileges

include membership in the church of Jesus Christ and being able to partake of the means of grace: prayer, the Word of God, and the sacraments (*Institutes* III:20; IV:14-19).

All persons are not children of God (*Commentary* on John 8:44). (Calvin would have nothing to do with the pseudo-Christian teaching of the brotherhood of all men and the universal fatherhood of God.) It is only those who are ingrafted into Christ, by means of the Spirit, that can call God "Abba Father." They are the co-heirs with Christ of the Father's Kingdom (*Commentary* on Romans 8:14-18).

Calvin also distinguishes between Christ's Sonship and the sonship of believers. It must not be forgotten that "he is the Son of God by nature, while we are the sons of God only by adoption." Nevertheless, this does not negate the richness of the relationship that Christians have with God the Father. For "he who is the God of Christ is their [believers'] God, and . . . he that is the Father of Christ is their Father" (*Commentary* on John 20:17,18).

7. Sanctification is "the work of God's free grace, whereby we are renewed in the whole man after the image of God, and are enabled more and more to die unto sin, and live unto righteousness."[8] With justification the guilt of sin is instantaneously eradicated, but with sanctification it is the pollution of sin which is progressively removed. Sanctification flows from justification. Says Calvin, "Christ justifies no one whom He does not sanctify at the same time" (*Institutes* III:16:1). God, in Christ, of course, is the author of both (*Commentary* on 1 Corinthians 1:30).

The whole of the Christian life concerns itself with sanctification. It is, states the Reformer, God's purpose for the Christian man during his earthly vigil (*Commentary* on 1 Thessalonians 4:3). The believer is called upon to deny himself (*i.e.,* the total resignation of one's life to the will of God, *Institutes* III:7), take up his cross daily for Christ's sake (*i.e.,* willingly sharing the sufferings of Christ, III:8), and live his life on this earth with a view toward eternal things (III:9,10). Calvin's doctrine of sanctification can be summarized as follows (*Institutes* III:3-20):

(a) Christians are positionally sanctified ("set apart") at the time of conversion. Yet, they must undergo the process of sanctification (*Commentary* on 1 Corinthians 1:2,3). And although the process is begun in this life, believers remain sinners until the time of their death (*Institutes* III:11:11).

(b) Sanctification speaks to both a separation from evil and a separation unto God (*Commentary* on 1 Thessalonians 4:3; John 10:36). Thus, Calvin maintains that true piety will find itself worked out in a two-fold fear of God: the Christian will tremble before him as Lord (a filial, not a servile fear), and reverence him as Father. The Christian man will embrace the righteousness of God, and dread offending him worse than death (*Institutes* III:2:26).

(c) In effectual calling, regeneration, justification, and adoption, the saint is wholly passive. But in sanctification he is active. He must work out his salvation in accordance with the Word of God. As noted, this involves self-denial: a total resignation of the whole man to the sovereign will of God (*Institutes* III:7:1-10). The entirety of the Christian man's life is to be involved in "mortification" (a dying to self and sin) and "vivification" (a holy seeking after the things of God) (III:3:3). In his *Commentary* on Jeremiah 20:8,9, Calvin warns against ever letting down one's guard in his striving against sin; a continual "burning heart" for God is necessary. But all the while the believer must recognize that it is God working in him, in the person of the Spirit, to accomplish his purpose (*Institutes* III:3:1-21; *Commentary* on Philippians 2:12,13).

(d) Sanctification affects the whole man; all of life is holy unto the Lord. This ongoing process of sanctification in the whole man is nothing more than a restoration of the ethical image of God in the Christian man (*Commentary* on Ephesians 4:22-24; Colossians 3:9,10; 1 Thessalonians 5:23; *Institutes* I:15:4).

Ronald Wallace points out that Calvin stresses the need for the Christian man to be involved in serious, daily Bible study and prayer. The promises given to the saints in Holy Scripture become the "fuel of prayer." The Spirit progressively works spiritual growth in the believer as he applies himself in this discipline. Prayer, which is the "chief exercise of faith," is greatly aided by a knowledge of the Psalms. Here the saints learn how the Old Covenant men of God poured out their hearts to God. According to Calvin, a non-praying, non-Bible study-ing Christian is a contradiction in terms.[9]

(e) Sanctification is to manifest itself in good works. The doctrine of justification by grace through faith does not eliminate the need of good works in the believer. "Christ justifies no one whom he does not at the same time sanctify"; and this sanctification manifests itself in the good works of the elect (*Institutes* III:16:1). Yet these good works are not the cause or ground of our justification, but the result (III:17:5; *Commentary* on James 2:25,26).

8. Perseverance and Assurance: "It cannot be," writes Calvin, "that the true members of the elect people of God should in the end perish or be lost."[10]

God, the author of salvation, by means of the Spirit will preserve his church; thus, all true members can be assured of their salvation (*Commentary* on Philippians 1:6). Says Calvin:

> In fine, when the Christian looks to himself he finds only occasion for trembling, or rather for despair; but having been called into the fellowship of Christ, he ought, in so far as assurance of salvation is concerned, to think of himself no otherwise than as a member of Christ, so as to reckon all Christ's benefits his own. Thus he will obtain an unwavering hope of final perseverance, (as it is called), if he reckons himself a member of him who is beyond hazard of falling away (*Commentary* on 1 Corinthians 1:9).

Calvin claims that the doctrine of perseverance is not one and the same thing with assurance. The doctrine of perseverance teaches that no Christian will finally fall away from the state of grace to which God has brought him. Yet, the individual's recognition of this in his own life may or may not be present; that is, it is possible that he may not have assurance. For instance, one may fall into heinous sin and doubt that he was ever saved in the first place. But this in no way negates the truth of the doctrine of perseverance (*Institutes* III:2:7,17-20). There is room in Calvin's doctrine for a weak, shaken, and diminished faith.

9. Glorification is the final state of salvation, wherein the elect pass into the presence of God at their death to everlasting bliss. This glory will be even further magnified at the resurrection on the last day (*Commentary* on Philippians 1:21-23; *Institutes* III:25:1-12). This will be further discussed in the chapter on eschatology.

CHAPTER NINE

CALVIN ON THE CHURCH

Calvin's contemporary, the German Reformer Martin Luther, once wrote:

> I believe that there is on earth, through the whole wide world, no more than one holy, common, Christian church, which is nothing else than the congregation, or the assembly of the saints, *i.e.*, the pious, believing men on earth, which is gathered, preserved, and ruled by the Holy Ghost, and daily increased by means of the sacraments and the Word of God.[1]

Calvin would fully agree. Calvin loved the church; she is the bride of Christ, the apple of God's eye. And he burned with a true zeal for her purification, reformation, and good health. In his *Commentary* on Galatians 5:12, Calvin writes, "my love of the church and my anxiety about her interests carry me away into a sort of ecstacy, so that I can think of nothing else."

As Louis Berkhof points out, Calvin and the Reformers broke with the Roman Catholic concept of an infallible and hierarchical church, a special priesthood, the saving nature of the sacraments, and so forth. Calvin, along with his mentor Augustine, held that there are four attributes of a true church: she is "one, holy, catholic [*i.e.*, universal], apostolic church." Moreover, along with these four attributes, there are three particular marks of the church: the true preaching of the Word, the proper administration of the sacraments, and the faithful exercise of church discipline. Further, there is the need to distinguish between the visible and the invisible church, and the church militant and triumphant.[2]

The Visible and Invisible Church

Calvin, with Augustine before him, and the Westminster Assembly after him, properly distinguishes between the visible and the invisible church (*Institutes* IV:1:7). The former consists of all those who have made a sincere profession of faith in Jesus Christ, and their children. The latter consists of all of the true saints (*i.e.*, the elect) of all time, even those not yet born. They are invisible to us because we are unable to search the hearts of man; but they are not invisible to God. It is this invisible church into which "Christ breathes . . . His own life and power" (*Commentary* on Ephesians 5:32). It is clear from his teaching on this subject that Calvin believed that Old Testament Israel was part and parcel of Christ's church (*Institutes* II:6:1-4).

True members of the visible church are, then, also members of the invisible church. But some who make a profession of faith and participate in the visible church are not truly saved. Thus, the visible church will ever remain, until the second advent of Christ, a "mixed body" of believers and non-believers (*Institutes* IV:1:13).

Calvin understood that the church was involved in holy warfare against the world, the flesh, and the devil. In this sense the bride of Christ is the church militant. In her own strength, she can never win the battle. It is only as the bride remains in the bridegroom, the "invincible" Lord Jesus Christ, that she can overcome. Nevertheless, the church is responsible to fight. Writes Calvin, "We shall not grow weary of fighting under the sign of the cross of our Lord Jesus Christ; for that is more valuable than all the victories of this world."[3] And during the struggle the church longs for the end, which the Lord will bring at the second advent in glory. At this time, the church will be the church triumphant. (Individual Christians, of course, become members of the church triumphant when they die.)

Calvin, with Augustine, taught that the church was the mother of all believers. Persons come to know Christ as Lord and Savior through the ministry of the church, and they continue to grow by means of grace in sanctification therein. In this sense, Calvin can say that outside the church there is no salvation (*Institutes* IV:1:1-4).

The Attributes of the Church

In the early years of Christendom, Augustine and the early church fathers affirmed that the church is "one, holy, catholic, apostolic" church. In the 1536 edition of the *Institutes*, Calvin's doctrine regarding the church, as found in the Fourth Part of his commentary on the Apostles Creed, shows that he is in accord with the early church:

1. *One:* The stress here is on the unity of the church. She is one bride of Christ. There is a "communion of the saints," with the individuals and the corporate body being in communion with Christ and one another. There exists within the church a corporate solidarity.

The apostle Paul, says Calvin, claims that there is a unity of the Spirit which exists within the Christian community, and yet there is a diversity of gifts which is necessary for the body to properly function. Diversity may exist without disunity (*Commentary* on Ephesians 4:1-16; 1 Corinthians 12).

With regard to the gifts, every Christian has a spiritual gift, which is to be used for the furtherance of God's Kingdom (*Commentary* on 1 Peter 4:10). But no Christian has all the gifts (*Commentary* on 1 Corinthians 12). The job of church pastors and teachers is to equip the saints, through the preaching and teaching of the Word of God, for ministry. As the laity is mobilized through the ministry of the Word, the whole body of saints is to become involved in the advancement of the Kingdom (*Commentary* on Ephesians 4:11,12).

2. *Holy:* The church consists of the saints (the *hagioi,* "sanctified ones") of God. They are sanctified by their Lord, Jesus Christ, being in union with him. In this way they are holy —they are "set apart" and chosen by God to participate in his church. Thus, the saints are also to pursue personal holiness (*Commentary* on Ephesians 1:1,2; 4:4-6; 5:22-23).

3. *Catholic:* This refers to the universal nature of the church in the New Covenant age. In Old Testament times the church was primarily restricted to the geo-political boundaries of the land of Canaan (but see Jonah 1:1,2; Nahum 1:1). However, since the death, burial, and resurrection of Jesus Christ, the church has become universal. That is, she is now meant to embrace all nations (*Commentary* on Matthew 28:18-20; Isaiah 54:1ff.).

4. *Apostolic:* The church is built on the foundation of Holy Scripture. As noted in the chapter on Scripture, Calvin did not hold to the continuation of the extraordinary gifts in the New Testament age. With the close of the canon, Scripture was complete. There are, therefore, no more apostles and prophets. But their message, as found solely in the canon of Scripture, continues. Here is the rock upon which the church stands (*Commentary* on Ephesians 2:20). Calvin states, "Paul testifies that the church is built on the foundation of the apostles and prophets" (*Institutes* I:7:2); the Word of God is the foundation of the church, not vice-versa (IV:2:4).

Ronald Wallace writes:

> [F]or Calvin the Bible is not only the sole source of church proclamation but also the sole authority that must rule the life of the church. . . . [T]hrough the preaching of the Word of God Christ rules within his church. . . . [T]his means that the Scripture is set over the church by God as the authority that must

be allowed full freedom to rule the life of the church.[4]

Here Calvin opposed the Roman Catholic dogma, which maintains that the church has authority over the Bible. In Roman Catholic theology, apostolic succession is carried out through the Papacy (or the Bishops), with an unbroken line traced back to Peter. Reformed and Calvinistic thinking, following John Calvin, asserts the continuity of apostolic teaching, not succession.

The Church and Worship

Public and corporate worship is a most important part of the biblical church. The saints are to gather together each and every Lord's Day to sing Psalms and other songs of praise, to pray, to study the Word of God, to partake of the sacraments, to give tithes and offerings, to exercise church discipline, and to recite the Apostles Creed (*Institutes* IV:17:43).[5]

In opposition to Catholicism, Calvin and the Reformed churches in general held to the "regulative principle of worship." That is, God is to be worshipped only in the manner which he has ordained in his Word (*Institutes* II:8:17). This Calvinistic principle is concisely set forth in the Westminster Confession of Faith (XXI:1):

> The acceptable way of worshipping the true God is instituted by himself, and so limited by his own revealed will, that he may not be worshipped according to the imaginations and devices of men, or the suggestions of Satan, under any visible representation, or any other way not prescribed in the Holy Scripture.

Calvin sees this principle being worked out in the apostolic church in Acts 2:42 (*Institutes* IV:17:44).

Calvin taught that the Christian's day of public worship is the Lord's Day, *i.e.*, Sunday. Much has been made over Calvin's continental view of the Christian Sabbath, which is not as strict as the Puritan view, as found in the Westminster Confession of Faith. It is true that the Reformer did teach that Christ, in his death, burial, and resurrection, had fulfilled the Jewish Sabbath, which was primarily ceremonial in import (*Institutes* II:8:28-34). But, as F. Nigel Lee has pointed out, Calvin also taught that in the New Testament age the Jewish Sabbath has been replaced by a Sunday Lord's Day.[6] Further, in his *Commentary* on Genesis 2:1-3, Calvin states that the Sabbath principle is "to continue to the end of the world."

The Relationship between Church and State

In the history of the church-state relationship, two major errors have developed: Papalism and Erastianism. The former teaches that the church (*i.e.,* the Pope) is to rule both church and state. The latter maintains that both institutions are under the headship of the civil magistrate. Calvin disavows both.

Biblical Christianity, says the Reformer, teaches that these two are separate God-ordained institutions, while at the same time they are both under his law (*i.e.,* there is a separation in function, but not in authority). In Romans 13:1-7, we read that civil rulers are God's ministers. Thus, it is incumbent upon civil magistrates to adopt the principles of civil law, *i.e.,* the Ten Commandments and the general equity of the Mosaic judicials, as found in Scripture. Likewise, the church is to be governed by Scriptural ecclesiastical law. The church wields only the sword of the Spirit in dealing with sin, whereas the state wields the sword of iron in accordance with Scripture, in dealing with crime. The state is not to administer the Word of God or the sacraments. It has no authority over the keys of the Kingdom. And the church is not to enter into the affairs of the civil government, other than for advice and counsel (*Institutes* IV:11:3; 20:1-13; *Commentary* on Romans 13:1-7).

Calvin taught that the office of civil magistrate was the highest "calling" that a Christian man could receive (*Institutes* IV:20:4). Yet so firmly did he adhere to the biblical separation of the two institutions of church and state that he decreed that the office of pastor should disqualify one from holding public office (except under the rarest of circumstances, *e.g.,* Moses) (IV:8:11).

The biblical separation of church and state, however, does not render them totally indifferent to one another. According to Calvin, the church is to pray for and uphold the magistrate, to teach the magistrate his biblical function, and to give rulers the honor due a biblical institution (and Calvin did so diligently). The magistrate is to promote the welfare of the true church, as well as all his subjects, and to guard her against her opponents. Both institutions are to work together for the advancement of God's Kingdom (*Institutes* IV:20:2,8).

Calvin distinguished the church from the Kingdom of God. The church is in the Kingdom and is mightily used by God in the furtherance of the Kingdom, but it is not the Kingdom. Louis Berkhof has rightly summarized Calvin's concept of the church and the Kingdom:

> [T]he visible church is instrumental in the establishment and extension of the Kingdom . . . [but] the Kingdom may be said to be a broader concept than the church, because it aims at nothing less than the complete control of all the manifestations of life. It represents the dominion of God in every sphere of human endeavor.[7]

In Calvin's view, the civil magistrate's duties are mainly relegated to those of justice and defense. The magistrate is to assure that there is no blasphemy, idolatry, disturbance of the peace, wronging of other's property, and so forth. At the same time, the Bible gives the state the power to punish crime and to take up arms against aggressor nations when necessary. As the magistrate carries out these functions, "it carries out the very judgments of God" (*Institutes* IV:20:3,10,11). This does not mean, however, that the civil magistrate exists as a necessary evil, because of sin. Rather, it exists as a holy aspect of God's righteous judgment (*Commentary* on Romans 13:1).

The Marks of the Church

In his *Institutes,* Calvin maintained that there are three essential marks of the church: the preaching of the Word of God, the proper administration of the sacraments, and biblical church discipline (IV:1:9; 12:1-13). (Calvin is somewhat inconsistent here in that in the first reference he states that there are only two marks [the first two mentioned above]. But in the latter reference he emphatically maintains that biblical church discipline is necessary for a church to be a church.)

1. The preaching of the Word of God: Calvin held that the church is built on the foundation of the Word of God. Thus, it is essential that the Word—the whole counsel of God—be proclaimed. It is by means of the gospel that individuals come to know Jesus Christ as Savior and Lord. And it is by means of the Word that they grow in sanctification (*Institutes* III:2:2,6,7,33; 3:1-3).

In opposition to Rome, Calvin and the Reformers stressed the preaching of the Word over the sacraments, because, they maintained, the Word is complete as a means of grace in itself. That is, the Bible is absolutely necessary for salvation under normal circumstances; but the sacraments, as important as they are, are a means of grace only when administered with the Word. One cannot even understand the meaning of the sacraments apart from the Word; thus, in a real sense, the Word of God creates the sacraments. The Word both begets and strengthens faith, whereas the sacraments merely strengthen it (*Institutes* IV:14:1-6).

Preaching is the instrument of Christ's rule over the church; it is a sign of God's presence.[8] Calvin writes that, "the scepter of his [Christ's] Kingdom is the gospel" (*Commentary* on Hosea 1:11). By means of preaching, Christ advances his Kingdom in this world; "he subdues the world to himself by the preaching of the gospel" (*Commentary* on Acts 1:8).

2. The proper administration of the sacraments: In the Geneva Confession (1536) Calvin writes:

> We believe that the sacraments which our Lord has ordained in his church are to be regarded as exercises of faith for us, both for fortifying and confirming it in the promises of God and for witnessing before men. Of them, there are only two which are instituted by the authority of our Savior: Baptism and the Supper of our Lord; for what is held within the realm of the pope concerning seven sacraments, we condemn as fable and lie.
>
> Baptism is an external sign by which our Lord testifies that he desires to receive us for his children, as members of his Son Jesus. Hence in it there is represented to us the cleansing from sin which we have in the blood of Jesus Christ, the mortification of our flesh which we have by his death that we may live in him by his Spirit. Now since our children belong to such an alliance with our Lord, we are certain that the external sign is rightly applied to them.
>
> The Supper of our Lord is a sign by which under bread and wine he represents the true spiritual communion which we have in his body and blood. And we acknowledge that according to his ordinance it ought to be distributed in the company of the faithful, in order that all those who wish to have Jesus for their life be partakers of it. Inasmuch as the mass of the pope was a reprobate and diabolical ordinance subverting the mystery of the Holy Supper, we declare that it is execrable to us, and idolatry condemned by God; for so much is it itself regarded as a sacrifice for the redemption of souls that the bread is in it taken and adored as God. Besides there are other execrable blasphemies and superstitions implied here, and the abuse of the Word of God which is taken in vain without profit or edification.[9]

Calvin has been quoted here at length for the purpose of showing, in one full statement, his overall view of the sacraments. In the foregoing comments, Calvin upholds the Protestant position that there are two sacraments with biblical authority, instead of Rome's seven. They are ordained by Christ himself and to be considered as necessary as a mark of the church.

Further, following Augustine, Calvin teaches that the sacraments are to be seen as "a visible form of an invisible grace" (*Institutes* IV:14:1). The sacraments are, in the words of the Westminster Assembly, "holy signs and seals of the covenant of grace." They are "sensible [*i.e.*, may be impressed upon the sensory organs] signs, [by which] Christ and the benefits of the New Covenant are represented, sealed, and applied to believers."[10] As covenant signs, then, the sacraments signify inward spiritual graces. And as seals, they attest to the genuineness or validity of the covenant promises of God.

However, as the sacraments are external signs and seals, they do not convey grace *ex opere operato* ("by the work performed") as in Roman Catholicism; neither are they absolutely necessary for salvation (*Institutes* IV:14:14-17). Calvin's theology of the sacraments also denies Rome's teaching of transubstantiation (*i.e.*, that the bread and wine are physically transformed into the body and blood of Christ), and Lutheranism's consubstantiation (*i.e.*, that Christ's body and blood are physically "contained" in the elements which remain bread and wine). (The fact that Christ's body is now in heaven refutes these two false positions.) To Calvin, the bread and wine remain bread and wine; and Christ's presence, as real as it is at the Supper, is a spiritual presence (*i.e.*, the body and blood of Christ are "spiritually contained" in the elements). Further, the Reformer denounces the Roman Catholic Mass as heretical (IV:14:14-17; 17:3,12,26).[11]

While the sacraments are outward signs and seals of inward graces, this does not mean that the participants do not receive Christ. On the contrary, Calvin agrees with the Westminster Assembly that, by the work of God's Spirit, "There is in every sacrament a spiritual relationship, or sacramental union, between the sign and the thing signified; whence it comes to pass, that the names and effects of the one are attributed to the other."[12]

Thus, he writes, "in the sacraments the reality is given to us along with the sign; for when the Lord holds out a sacrament, he does not feed our eyes with an empty and unmeaning figure, but joins the truth with it. . . . [W]e ought to believe that [the truth] must never be separated from the signs, though it ought to be distinguished from them." In the sacraments, believers have fellowship with Christ by means of the Spirit. Here they receive the whole Christ; they feed on him, spiritually. Grace is therefore represented, sealed and applied to those "in faith" by the Spirit (*Commentary* on Isaiah 6:7).[13]

Baptism, says Calvin, is a sign and seal of one's entering into a covenant relationship with God (as in regeneration); thus, it is only to be administered once, by immersion, sprinkling, or pouring (*Institutes* IV:18:19; 15:18,19). In water baptism, the outward sign (water) points to true baptism, which is the work of the Holy Spirit (*Commentary* on Acts 1:5).

The Lord's Supper, on the other hand, is a covenant sign and seal of one's continuing in his covenant relationship with God, as in sanctification (*Institutes* IV:18:19); thus, it should be taken frequently, preferably each and every week (IV:17:43). In this sacrament, the outward signs of bread and wine symbolize the body and blood of the Lord Jesus. And, says Calvin, in accordance with John 6, "his flesh is truly food . . . his blood is truly drink . . . none shall have life except those who eat his flesh and drink his blood" (IV:17:7).

Because children of believers are members of the covenant, they should be baptized in infancy (*Commentary* on 1 Corinthians 7:14). This is in accordance with the covenant which God established with Abraham, that covenant in which all believers and their seed participate (*Institutes* IV:16:6; *Commentary* on Matthew 28:19). The Lord's Supper, on the other hand, is for believers only. It is for those who are capable of self-examination; thus, children are forbidden to come to the table until they can examine themselves (*Institutes* IV:16:30; *Commentary* on 1 Corinthians 11:23ff.).

Finally, it should be noted that Calvin maintained that the sacraments were graciously given by God to his people as a teaching device. As a visible (and sensible) means of grace, the sacraments aid us in our human weakness. He writes:

> For God's truth is of itself firm and sure enough, and it cannot receive better confirmation from any other source than from itself. But as our faith is slight and feeble unless it be propped on all sides and sustained by every means, it trembles, wavers, totters, and at last gives way. Here our merciful Lord, according to His infinite kindness, so tempers Himself to our capacity that, since we are creatures who always creep on the ground, cleave to the flesh, and, do not think about or even conceive of anything spiritual, He condescends to lead us to Himself even by these earthly elements [*i.e.*, the sacraments], and to set before us in the flesh a mirror of spiritual blessings (*Institutes* IV:14:3).

3. Church discipline: The church is called on to oversee each and every one of her members. As the leaders faithfully preach the Word and properly administer the sacraments, positive church discipline is carried out. Sometimes, however, these leaders and members find themselves in sin which must be dealt with. In Matthew 18:15-20, the Lord gave his church directions for such (negative) church discipline.

There is a three-fold step to the disciplinary process. First, the sinner is to be approached alone. If this step does not bring repentance, then there are to be witnesses taken in the second phase. Finally, if there is still no repentance, the matter is to be handled at the congregational level (*Commentary* on Matthew 18:15-20).

Whenever, says Calvin, repentance is manifested in the process, the sinner is to be forgiven and restored to fellowship within the church. If there is no repentance witnessed, the final result is excommunication. Church discipline has three purposes: the glory of God, the purity of the church, and the restoration of the sinner (*Institutes* IV:12:1-7). The discipline carried out by church courts, of course, can only judge the outward behavior of persons. The inner man is known only to the individual and God (*Commentary* on 1 Corinthians 5:11; *Institutes* IV:12:6).

Calvin, of course, did not enjoy church discipline. But as it is a biblical mandate, he recognized the need to carry it out. He was firmly convinced that where there is no discipline, there is no church. He writes, "The collapse of the church would surely follow unless the preaching of doctrine was supported by private admonitions, corrections, and other aids of the sort that sustain doctrine and do not let it remain idle" (*Institutes* IV:12:1).

And for Calvin, unlike Luther, church discipline was strictly "church business." The civil rulers were to exercise no oversight of that which took place within Christ's church (*Institutes* IV:20:1; 11:3).

Church Government

The church is an organization. Therefore, it needs a governmental structure. A church without government cannot function. Paul speaks to this need for orderliness in 1 Corinthians 14:40 (*Institutes* IV:3:10).

Over the centuries there have been three basic forms of church government: episcopal (or hierarchical), independent (or congregational), and presbyterian. It is, of course, true that some churches, such as the Quakers and the Plymouth Brethren, reject all church government. But, in fact, some of these do elect leaders and exercise discipline.

The episcopal form of government, as found in Roman Catholic, Episcopalian, Anglican, and Methodist churches, with various degrees of authority resting with the Bishop (Rome is the most centralized, with the Papacy), holds that the church is to be governed by the Bishop *(episkopos)*. Independent churches hold to the fundamental principle that the local congregation is independent from any other churches; it is complete in itself. Each church is to be governed democratically. The church is run by majority vote of the congregation. Calvin opposed both of these. He was Presbyterian *(Institutes* IV:4-13).

Calvin taught that the presbyterian form of government was the most biblical. (He was strongly opposed to huge bureaucratic structures.) Here the elders *(presbuteroi),* having been elected by the congregation, govern the church under the headship of Jesus Christ *(Institutes* IV:3:1-16, *Commentary* on 1 Peter 5:1-4; Acts 14:23). The Word of God vests this ruling authority in men alone, who are gifted by his Spirit to serve *(Commentary* on 1 Timothy 2:11-3:16; *Institutes* IV:11:1).

The presbyterian form of church government, says Calvin, was founded, in principle, in the Old Testament *(Commentary* on Exodus 18:13ff; Numbers 11:16ff.). It was then implemented by the apostles in the New *(Institutes* IV:3:1-16). Moreover, it has been the biblical government used within the true church since the days of the apostles. Within this system of government, there is a series of church courts: at the local level there is the session (or consistory); next is the presbytery (or classis) level (at this level, "The Company of Pastors of Geneva" would regularly meet and examine candidates for the ministry); then finally, there is the general assembly or synod (the highest church court), which should meet only on certain occasions *(i.e.,* infrequently) *(Institutes* IV:8,9; *Commentary* on Acts 15:6). According to Calvin, it was Roman Catholicism which later corrupted biblical presbyterianism *(Institutes* IV:5-7).

In his *Draft Ecclesiastical Ordinances* of 1541, as we saw in his *Institutes* (IV:3,4), Calvin maintained that there were four basic orders of offices within the church: pastors, doctors (teachers), elders, and deacons. These officers were to be elected by the people to rule over and serve them.

1. *Pastor:* This office is sometimes also referred to in the Bible as overseer, elder, and minister. The duties of the pastor include preaching, teaching, administering the sacraments, admonishing and reproving, both privately and publicly, and shepherding the flock, along with the other (ruling) elders. Due to his special charge to administer the Word and the sacraments, the pastor, according to Calvin, is to have a special, unique relationship with the flock. Under Christ, he is the "chief sinew" which holds the body of believers together (*Institutes* IV:3:1,2; *Commentary* on Titus 1:5).

2. *Doctor:* This office is primarily one of teaching. It is somewhat closely allied with that of the pastor. A church doctor would assist in teaching the people the Word of God, training future ministers, teaching at the college, testing the wholesomeness of the current ministry of the Word, etc. But he did not normally administer the sacraments; hence, this office was secondary in importance to that of the pastor (*Commentary* on Romans 12:6-8; Ephesians 4:11).

3. *Elder:* This officer functioned as a ruling elder, and along with the pastor (the teaching elder), he would shepherd the flock under the care of the local church. This would involve church discipline, both positive and negative (*Institutes* IV:3:8). In his *Commentary* on Acts 20:20, Calvin speaks to the need of the pastor and the elders to go from "house to house" in their shepherding responsibilities.

4. *Deacon:* This office was intimately involved in the ministry of mercy. There were to be two kinds of deacons: "the one to receive, distribute and care for the goods of the poor (*i.e.,* daily alms as well as possessions, rents, and pensions); the other has to tend and look after the sick and administer the allowances to the poor as is customary."[14] Women could be used to help in this second function (although they could not hold church office). For Calvin, the social welfare concerns of society were to be handled by the church, not by the civil magistrate. The Reformer viewed this as a diaconal function.[15]

CHAPTER TEN

CALVIN ON THE LAST THINGS

Eschatology is the study of the doctrine of the "last things" (from the Greek *eschatos,* meaning "last"). This study is normally subdivided into individual (or personal) and general (or cosmic) eschatology. The former examines the phenomenon of death and the "intermediate" state, as it applies to individuals. The latter studies those events which are to occur at the close of human history; it includes the millennium, the general resurrection and judgment, and the eternal state.

Calvin's view of eschatology (both personal and general) is inextricably related to his concept of history. His is a dynamic view of history in which the sovereign, predestinating God of Scripture is actively involved, not only in creating all things, but also in providentially bringing all of history to its appointed destiny (*Institutes* I:16:3). With the first coming of Christ and the irruption of the first phase of his Kingdom into history, God has summed up all things (*Commentary* on Ephesians 1:9,10). Now, like that great stone which Daniel envisioned (2:31-45), Christ's Kingdom is progressively rolling along, crushing the other world kingdoms, until it reaches its ultimate state in glory. This Kingdom will have no end (*Commentary* on Daniel 2:31ff.).[1] Thus, we can say that Calvin's eschatology is predominantly Christocentric. For him, the message of Christ is the center of all Scripture.

Individual Eschatology

Man was created upright by God. If Adam had not sinned, he would have lived forever. But at the fall, man, in Adam, lost this status. The body now must undergo physical death, and the soul, which is immortal, spiritual death (*i.e.*, separation from the grace of God) (*Commentary* on Genesis 2:16,17; Romans 5:12ff.).

Death, therefore, is not natural to man. It is God's curse on disobedience. For believers, however, the curse is removed. They still must die, but they die in Christ, who took the curse on their behalf (*Commentary* on Matthew 26:36-39; Hebrews 2:15). Death is, then, for the Christian man, a conquered foe. In faith he can face death, understanding its cursedness and acknowledging it as a judgment on sin; yet, in Christ, he can face it (and even long for death [*Institutes* III:9:4]) as a blessing to be desired.[2]

At death, a man's body returns to the dust and sees corruption and decay, but the soul, the man himself, enters into the intermediate state and maintains consciousness. Here there is a vast difference between Christian and non-Christian man. Commenting on Jesus' parable of Lazarus and the rich man, Calvin says:

> The general truth conveyed is that believing souls, when they have left their bodies, lead a joyful and blessed life out of this world, and that for the reprobate there are prepared dreadful torments, which can no more be conceived by our minds than the boundless glory of the heavens (*Commentary* on Luke 16:23).

Calvin's exegesis of the parable of Lazarus and the rich man also condemns, either explicitly or implicitly, "re-incarnation," "soul sleep," "annihilationism," and "conditional immortality" (*Commentary* on Luke 16:19-31). As noted in an earlier chapter, Calvin's first major theological work, *Psychopannychia*, taught the immortality of the soul and refuted the false doctrines mentioned above.

As seen, the intermediate state is one "without body." The Bible views this incorporeal condition as temporary, although it may last thousands of years, much longer than one's life on earth. The eternal state will be one in which men will once again have bodies; they will have "the self-same [glorified] bodies . . . which shall be united again to their souls forever"[3] (*Commentary* on 2 Corinthians 5:1,2; *Institutes* III:25:1-7). Calvin, in his *Commentary* on 2 Corinthians 5:4, states that the souls of believers are now "shut up in a body as in a prison . . . in it they cannot enjoy true and perfect blessedness." But our glorified bodies, says Calvin, will be as mansions, not prisons.

In the intermediate state, both believers and unbelievers await the final, general resurrection and judgment which will occur at the second advent of Christ. It is on this day that "The bodies of the unjust shall, by the power of Christ, be raised to dishonour; [and] the bodies of the just, by his Spirit, unto honour, and made conformable to His own glorious body."[4] This final state of the righteous will be more glorious than that of the intermediate state, while the state of the unrighteous will be far worse (*Institutes* III:25:1-12; *Commentary* on Matthew 25:31-46).

Calvin's doctrine of personal eschatology called upon him to spend much time meditating on the future life. By so meditating, the Christian man learns, not only to live well, but to die well. He writes, "We are God's: let us therefore live for Him and die for Him. We are God's: let all the parts of our life accordingly strive toward Him as our lawful goal" (*Institutes* III:7:1).

General Eschatology

According to Calvin, the Bible teaches that at his first advent, Jesus Christ established his mediatorial Kingdom. Yet, the Bible also teaches that there is a future aspect to this Kingdom, which will be manifested at the second coming.

Whereas the Old Testament viewed the coming Kingdom as one undivided whole, the New Covenant reveals that there are two stages. The first phase is the Kingdom of grace, the second the Kingdom of glory (*Commentary* on Isaiah 2:2-4; 65:17; Matthew 25:31).

In principle, the world has already been redeemed. But the complete expulsion of evil awaits Christ's return in glory. History entered into its final days at the first advent. The time of the consummation of the ages has begun. Yet, there is still the final stage to come—"the last day." We now live in the "present age," and await the "age to come."

In the period between the first and second comings of Christ, the church is carrying out the great commission of Matthew 28:18-20. The Kingdom of God is advancing; the enemies of Christ are being subdued under his feet by the work of his church. This Kingdom growth, according to Calvin, is making great progress toward the renovation of the whole world. But this will not fully occur until the Kingdom of glory (*Commentary* on Matthew 24:29; Luke 17:20).[5]

Calvin is claimed by advocates of both postmillennialism and amillennialism. He was not a premillennialist: This doctrine of the "chiliasts," he says, is "too childish either to need or to be worth a refutation" (*Institutes* III:25:5; see also *Commentary* on 1 Thessalonians 4:17).

Some postmillennialsts have called Calvin's millennial view "incipient postmillennialism." Others refer to him as an "optimistic" amillennialist. On the one hand, the Reformer, in a sermon on Isaiah 52:13-53:1, categorically denied that the world would ever be fully Christianized prior to the second advent. Neither does he teach that Romans 11 requires a future conversion of the Jews (*Commentary* on Romans 11:11ff.). On the other hand, he is very optimistic regarding Kingdom growth. In fact, the second generation of Reformers, and the overwhelming majority of Puritans, taking their lead from Calvin's optimism, became strong advocates of postmillennialism.

This optimism concerning Kingdom growth can be found in several *Commentaries*. On Psalm 47, he claims that Christ's Kingdom is to grow to the point where all nations will be included. The same is true of his exposition of Psalm 72. Yet, says the Reformer, there will always be opposition to the Kingdom (*Commentary* on Psalm 110:1). Just prior to the second coming of Christ there will be a great apostasy.

As stated earlier, at the end of this present age, Christ will come again, will resurrect all mankind and sit as judge of the nations (*Commentary* on Matthew 25:31ff.). On that day, the just will be raised unto a resurrection of utter blessedness, but the unjust will be raised unto dishonor. The sheep and the goats will be separated. This day is the "blessed hope" of all Christian men, but it is that day when all of the ungodly will be finally "cut off" from even the unsaving grace of God which they experience in the present age. God's awesome wrath will be their lot forever (*Institutes* III:25:1-12).

Calvin, with many of the Reformers and later Puritans,[6] maintained that the Papacy was the Antichrist referred to by Paul in 2 Thessalonians 2. Various of the past Roman emperors, and others, may have been Antichrists of a fashion, but "the Antichrist" was the Papacy. And, said Calvin, the sixteenth century church was witnessing the fulfillment of Paul's prophecy with its own eyes. Nevertheless, the Reformer expected a greater success of the gospel prior to the second advent of Christ. Thus, he taught that the Word of God would have great success in the overthrow of Papal power, but the total expunging of this anti-Christian force would not occur until Christ's second coming, immediately subsequent to a time of great apostasy within the church (*Commentary* on 2 Thessalonians 2:3-11).

Although Calvin did not hold to the doctrine of the imminent return of Christ, he did teach that a life lived constantly focused on the second advent would prevent apathy and slothfulness in the Christian man (*Commentary* on 2 Peter

3:9,10). Here, once again, Calvin finds himself in agreement with the Westminster divines, who maintained that:

> As Christ would have us to be certainly persuaded that there shall be a day of judgment, both to deter all men from sin; and for the greater consolation of the godly in their adversity: so will he have that day unknown to men, that they may shake off all carnal security, and be always watchful, because they know not at what hour the Lord will come; and may be ever prepared to say, Come, Lord Jesus, come quickly, Amen.[7]

Notes

Chapter One: The Man, The Churchman, and the Statesman

1. *Institutes* II:2:12-17; see also R.C. Sproul, *Pleasing God*, pp. 66, 67.
2. William Wileman, *John Calvin: His Life, His Teaching, and His Influence*, p. 11.
3. Wileman, p. 85.
4. John Gerstner, *Handout Church History*, p. 24.
5. Benjamin B. Warfield, *Calvin and Augustine*, p. 8.
6. *Calvin and Calvinism*, p. 374.
7. Philip Schaff, *History of the Christian Church*, Vol. VII, p. 32.
8. Cited in R.J. Rushdoony, *Politics of Guilt and Pity*, p. 269.
9. Ronald Wallace, *Calvin, Geneva and the Reformation*, p. 16.
10. Frank C. Roberts, *To All Generations*, p. 161.
11. J.H. Alexander, *Ladies of the Reformation*, pp. 92, 93.
12. *John Calvin*, John Dillenberger, editor, p. 5.
13. Roberts, p. 165.
14. Dillenberger, p. 9.
15. Dillenberger, p. 11.
16. F. Nigel Lee, *John Calvin: True Presbyterian*, p. 20.
17. Gregg Singer, *John Calvin: His Roots and Fruits*, pp. 29-32.
18. Singer, pp. 21, 22.
19. Wileman, p. 98.
20. Wileman, p. 106.
21. *Calvin: Theological Treatises*, J.K.S. Reid, editor, pp. 35-37, 58-72.
22. Wallace, pp. 291-293.
23. Lee, pp. 10, 11.
24. Cited in Wileman, p. 136.
25. Wallace, p. 300.
26. See also the *Institutes* I:9, 10; IV:5-8.
27. Wileman, pp. 127, 128, 130, 135.

28. *Catechism* (1537), cited by Ford Lewis Battles, "True Piety According to Calvin," *Readings in Calvin's Theology,* edited by Donald K. McKim, p. 192.
29. Robert Peterson, *Calvin's Doctrine of the Atonement,* pp. 83, 84.
30. Wallace, p. 28.
31. Singer, pp. 40, 41.
32. Wallace, pp. 89-96.
33. Leland Ryken, *Worldly Saints,* pp. 23-36. See Max Weber, *The Protestant Ethic and the Spirit of Capitalism.*
34. Singer, pp. 56-60.
35. Singer, pp. 65-69.

Chapter Two: Calvin on Knowledge

1. B.B. Warfield, *Calvin and Augustine,* p. 117.
2. B.B. Warfield might take issue with this statement *(Calvin and Augustine,* pp. 29-130), as would R.C. Sproul, John Gerstner, and Arthur Lindsley *(Classical Apologetics,* pp. 198-208). They would maintain that Calvin thought of the evidences as working together with the testimony of the Spirit; thus, he would use them as inductive arguments. The problem here is that all inductive arguments are logical fallacies. Even in the Garden before the fall, man was dependent on propositional revelation for knowledge. He could not, by observation, have determined where he was or what he was to do. God had to tell him then, and the present situation, exacerbated by sin, is worse. For example, in his *Commentary* on Exodus 4:5, Calvin asserts that miracles, as a biblical evidence, are used, "sometimes . . . as preparatives to faith, sometimes for its confirmation." They can be used to "open a door of faith." But they are only to be presented as the biblical evidences of the God of Scripture, and never as proof.
3. *History of the Christian Church,* Vol. VII, p. 32.
4. Gregg Singer, *John Calvin, His Roots and Fruits,* pp. 52-55.

Chapter Three: Calvin on Scripture

1. Westminster Confession of Faith, I:6.
2. B.B. Warfield, *Calvin and Augustine,* pp. 82, 83.
3. Cited in *Table Talk,* March 1991, p. 10.
4. Neo-orthodoxy maintains that parts of the Bible become the Word of God —different parts for different hearers at different times; the Bible is not "the Word of God." Karl Barth and Emil Brunner, two champions of neo-orthodoxy, for example, taught that the only true revelation of God to man is Jesus Christ (the Word of God Incarnate), and when Scripture

"reveals" Christ to the reader, then the Bible becomes God's Word. According to Barth and Brunner, it was beneath God, who is "wholly other," to communicate the trancendental Christ through logical propositions. Thus, God reveals events to us in the Bible, but not the meaning of the events. The understanding of the meaning is a subjective enterprise. Neo-orthodoxy, then, in claiming that revelation is merely an event (*i.e.,* something that happens), denies that the Bible gives us propositional revelation (see Robert L. Reymond, *Introductory Studies in Contemporary Theology,* pp. 91ff.; Ronald H. Nash, *The Word of God and the Mind of Man,* pp. 35ff.).

Further, in neo-orthodox theology, the Bible contains errors. It was written by fallen men and is full of logical paradoxes (as distinguished from rhetorical paradoxes) and contradictions. Brunner goes so far at one point as to claim that contradiction is the hallmark of religious truth (cited in John Gerstner, *Jonathan Edwards: A Mini-Theology,* p. 24). Thus, neo-orthodoxy is called the "Theology of Paradox" (R.V. Schnucker, *Evangelical Dictionary of Theology,* Walter A. Elwell, editor, pp. 754-756, 827).

According to the Genevan Reformer, nothing could be more nonsensical. Calvin maintained, along with all orthodoxy, that the Bible teaches propositional truth. Propositions are logical, understandable combinations of words which teach something. They are the meaning of indicative sentences. The truth of Scripture is not "in between" or "above" the words, or only in the mind of the interpreter. Neither are the words secretly symbolic, merely intimating some higher truth. Rather, God's truth lies in the logical meaning and organization of the words themselves. His truth comes via our understanding of these propositions according to the rules of grammar and logic. Thus, the Bible does not contain logical paradoxes. Just because something in Scripture might "exceed [our] mental capacity," says Calvin, does not make it paradoxical. "For our wisdom ought to be nothing else than to embrace with humble teachableness . . . without finding fault, whatever is taught in sacred Scripture" (*Institutes* I:18:4). Calvin might have agreed with Gordon Clark's definition of paradox as "a charley-horse between the ears that can be eliminated by rational massage" (*The Atonement,* p. 32).

This also relates to the events of history and their meaning. That is, not only does the Bible teach us that certain events occurred in history, but it also tells us what those events mean. The interpretation is not subjective; God reveals the meaning to the reader in his Word. That this is Calvin's view of Scripture is irrefutable (*Institutes* I:6-10; *Commentary* on 2 Timothy 3:16). In the opinion of this author, the claims of Wilhelm Niesel that Calvin was basically neo-orthodox in his view of Scripture are unfounded (*The Theology of Calvin*, pp. 22ff.). E.J. Young concurs: "How different is this modern view [neo-orthodoxy] and that . . . of Calvin! Calvin would have reacted with all his being against this false idea that the Bible and the Word of God are not to be identified" (*Thy Word is Truth*, p. 232).

5. William Wileman, *John Calvin: His Life, His Teaching, and His Influence*, p. 124.

6. Warfield, pp. 63, 64.

7. E.J. Young, *Thy Word Is Truth*, pp. 66. 67. John Gerstner affirms that various Puritans, such as Jonathan Edwards, likewise used the word "dictate" when referring to the inspiration of Scripture. But in using this term, they did not speak to the means by which Scripture was written, but to the end product, which was nothing other than the very words which God intended (*The Rational Biblical Theology of Jonathan Edwards*, Vol. I, pp. 140-145).

8. John Murray points out that some have maintained that Calvin did not hold to a high view of verbal, plenary inspiration, due to his somewhat cavalier comments on such passages as Matthew 27:9; Acts 7:14-16; and Hebrews 11:21. In commenting on Matthew 27:9, for example, Calvin speaks of the name of Jeremiah somehow mistakenly "creeping into the text" of Matthew's gospel; neither, says the Reformer, does he much concern himself over the matter. But here, as Murray points out, Calvin is merely referring to a textual error which occurred through the pen of some copyist; he is in no way to be considered as speaking of the original writing (*Calvin on Scripture and Divine Sovereignty*, pp. 11-13.)

But, says Murray, an overview of his writings will show that, "In Calvin we have a mass of perspicuous statements and of lengthened argument to the effect that Scripture is impregnable and inviolable, and it would be the resort of desperation to take a few random comments, wrench them from the total effect of Calvin's teaching, and build upon them a thesis which would run counter to his own repeated assertions respecting the inviolable character of Scripture as the oracle of God and as having nothing human mixed with it" (p. 31). Murray cites such men as E.A. Dowey, "There is no hint anywhere in Calvin's writings that the original text contained any flaws at all," and Kenneth S. Kantzer, "[Calvin held to] a rigidly orthodox verbal type of inspiration," to support his statement (pp. 11, 12).

Gordon Clark is in agreement with Murray. In *The Concept of Biblical Authority*, Clark cites Paul Rees as teaching that Calvin (as well as Augustine and Luther) was far from orthodox in his view of Scripture. But, notes Clark, "To cite Calvin as a witness to, a precursor of, or an exponent of a theory of biblical fallibility is unwarranted" (p. 10).

Likewise, Gregg Singer claims that, "There can be no doubt that Calvin regarded the men who wrote the Bible as the organs of the Holy Spirit, who guided them to write in such a way that they were without error of any kind. . . . [I]n his *Institutes*, his commentaries and his many writings, there is an abundance of evidence . . . [which points to] one inescapable fact: Calvin believed that the Bible is the uniquely inspired Word of God and that, as such, it differs in kind from all other literature" (*John Calvin: His Roots and Fruits*, pp. 8, 9).

Further, the paucity of documents from the pen of Calvin taking a strong stand on the subject of biblical inerrancy and infallibility has led others to deny what Murray, Clark, and Singer have maintained regarding the Reformer's view of Scripture. But this, according to John Gerstner, is easily explainable. In the sixteenth century, says Gerstner, biblical inerrancy was taken for granted by Roman Catholic and Protestant theologians alike. In Calvin's day, this doctrine was not in question. Thus, there was little need to write on the subject (*Christian Observer*, July 6, 1990, Vol. 168, Number 27, p.10).

9. Ronald S. Wallace, *Calvin's Doctrine of the Word and Sacrament*, pp. 106-114.

10. Singer, p. 10.

11. Reformed theology in general has always maintained that the extraordinary offices of the first century church (apostles and prophets) and the miraculous word gifts which accompanied them (prophecy, tongues, etc.) passed away with the close of the canon (1 Corinthians 13:8-13; Westminster Confession of Faith I:1:2; Sinclair Ferguson, *John Owen on the Christian Life*, pp. 204-210).

This was also Calvin's teaching. For example, in his "Prefatory Address to King Francis I of France," which introduces the *Institutes*, Calvin clearly states that miracles were for the purpose of confirming the message and messenger of special revelation. He writes, "in demanding miracles of us, they [certain antagonists] act dishonestly. For we are not forging some new gospel, but are retaining that very gospel whose truth all the miracles of Jesus Christ and his disciples ever wrought to confirm." Thus, when special revelation ceased, so did the age of miracles. It is unreasonable to believe in continuing miracles when divine, special revelation has been canonized (B.B. Warfield, *Counterfeit Miracles*, p. 27).

There are, however, some places where the Reformer seems to have another opinion. Calvin does, for example, refer to the ongoing gift of prophecy in various writings (*Institutes* IV:3:4; *Commentary* on Romans 12:6 and 1 Corinthians 12:28). But when these are studied in context, and compared with his other writings, it seems obvious that he is speaking of the gift of prophecy, not as receiving new, direct revelation from God, but of the ongoing ministry of the preaching of the Word.

12. Wallace, p. 99. Calvin and the Reformers, and the Westminster Assembly after them, rejected the Apocryphal writings (and the Pseudepigrapha) as non-canonical. They recognized that these books were replete with doctrinal, ethical, and historical errors. Nevertheless, the Reformers, in general, did not deny the usefulness of reading through these books; they merely did not seek to give them the same place as "inspired Scripture" (Greg Bahnsen, *Antithesis*, September/October 1991, p. 45; D.H. Wallace, *Evangelical Dictionary of Theology*, Walter A. Elwell, editor, pp. 66, 67).

13. Murray, p. 50.

14. From the *Opera Selecta*, cited in Wallace, p. 85.

15. Donald K. McKim, "Calvin's View of Scripture," *Readings in Calvin's Theology*, Donald K. McKim, editor, pp. 64, 65.

16. *Collected Writings*, Vol. I, p. 308.

17. Singer, p. vi.

18. Singer, p. 7.

19. From "Calvin's Exegetical Principles," cited in McKim, p. 66.

20. Cited in Murray, pp. 309, 310.

21. Wileman, p. 83.

22. Frank Roberts, *To All Generations*, p. 165; see also Singer, pp. 62-64.

23. *History of the Christian Church*, Vol. VIII, p. 792.

24. Some scholars have denied Calvin's strong adherence to the Mosaic laws in matters of the civil magistrate due to several statements that he makes in the *Institutes* (IV:20:14-21), which would seemingly deny what has been stated in this chapter. But investigation of this section of the *Institutes* will reveal that what Calvin is opposed to is not the civil magistrate's responsibility to obey God's law as its standard, but the view of the Anabaptists that one had the right to rebel against any government which did not perfectly follow the biblical pattern for civil law. That this is Calvin's point is clear from the Prefatory Address to Francis I at the very beginning of the *Institutes*. Christianity, says the Reformer, is not a subversive, revolutionary religion. It is not subversive or revolutionary even though the civil ruler may not be enforcing biblical law.

Chapter Four: Calvin on God

1. Gregg Singer, *John Calvin: His Roots and Fruits*, p. 11.

2. *Selected Works of John Calvin*, Beveridge and Bonnet, editors, Vol. I, p. 33.

3. Cited in *Calvin: Theological Treatises,* J.K.S. Reid, editor, p. 26.
4. Robert L. Reymond, *God and Man in Holy Scripture,* p. 27.
5. Cited in Beveridge and Bonnet, Vol. II, p. 39.
6. B.B. Warfield, with characteristic brilliance, fully supports Calvin at this point. He even claims that the Reformer is the one who brought the church out of its implicit subordinationist Christology (*Biblical and Theological Studies,* pp. 58, 59).
7. Calvin here clearly sets forth his answer to the theological question, "Does God do things because they are 'just,' or are the things he does 'just' because he does them?" Manifestly, says the Reformer, the latter is the case. To opt for the former would be to affirm a law above God. God is sovereign; therefore, whatever he does is perfectly "just" simply because he does it. In Calvin's theology the Lawgiver is supreme; he is above the law, *ex lex,* not under the law, *sub lego.*
8. Westminster Confession of Faith, III:8.
9. Cited in Ronald Wallace, *Calvin, Geneva and the Reformation,* p. 272.
10. This is also the position of the Westminster Assembly (Westminster Confession of Faith, IV:2).
11. *Corpus Reformatorum,* cited in Wilhelm Niesel, *The Theology of Calvin,* p. 70.
12. *Readings in Calvin's Theology,* Donald K. McKim, editor, pp. 69, 70.
13. J.I. Packer, *A Quest for Godliness,* p. 129.
14. The Westminster Confession of Faith, V:4. This form of Calvinism is sometimes referred to as Christian determinism. For example, in his *Institutes* (I:16:8), Calvin writes, "we make God the ruler and governor of all things, who in accordance with His wisdom has from the farthest limit of eternity decreed what He was going to do, and now by His might carried out what He has decreed. From this we declare that not only heaven and earth and the inanimate creatures, but also the plans and intentions of men, are so governed by His providence that they are borne by it straight to their appointed end."
15. Cited in Partee, *Readings in Calvin's Theology,* p. 79.

Chapter Five: Calvin on Man

1. Brian Gerrish, "The Mirror of God's Goodness," in *Readings in Calvin's Theology,* Donald K. McKim, editor, pp. 107ff.
2. Wilhelm Niesel, *The Theology of Calvin,* pp. 64-69.
3. R.J. Rushdoony, *By What Standard?* pp. 131-133.
4. Gerrish, pp. 120-122.
5. G.C. Berkouwer, *Man: The Image of God,* pp. 194-233.

6. C.I. Scofield, *The Scofield Reference Bible,* note on 1 Thessalonians 5:23.
7. John Gerstner, *The Rational Biblical Theology of Jonathan Edwards,* Vol. I, pp. 544, 545.
8. Gerrish, p. 109.

Chapter Six: Calvin on the Covenant

1. Louis Berkhof states that even as early as Augustine (354-430) the concept of covenant theology is evident. But it was Johannes Cocceius (1603-1669) who really refined the doctrine (Louis Berkhof, *Systematic Theology,* pp. 211, 212, 265).
2. *New Dictionary of Theology,* Sinclair Ferguson, David Wright, and J.I. Packer, editors, p. 175.
3. Carl W. Bogue, *The Genesis Covenants,* p. 3.
4. *Readings in Calvin's Theology,* Donald McKim, editor, pp. 89-91.
5. Sinclair Ferguson, *John Owen on the Christian Life,* pp. 20, 21.
6. John Gerstner, *Handout Church History,* p. 32; Osterhaven, "Calvin on the Covenant," *Readings in Calvin's Theology,* pp. 89-91.
7. Gerstner, p. 32.
8. See Leon Morris, *The Apostolic Preaching of the Cross,* pp. 86ff.
9. In Calvin's covenant theology there is an absence of specific writing about a covenant of redemption. Later Reformed scholars refer to this covenant as one which occurred within the Triune Godhead, before the foundation of the world, wherein God the Father covenanted with God the Son to redeem fallen elect sinners. The covenant of redemption is foundational to the covenant of grace, which occurred in space-time history (Louis Berkhof, *Systematic Theology,* pp. 265ff.). However, even though the Reformer did not directly refer to this covenant of redemption, the concept is at least implicit in his supralapsarian view of the order of God's eternal decrees (*i.e.,* God's decree to elect teleologically preceded his decree to cause the fall) (*Commentary* on Malachi 1:2-6; *Institutes* II:12:5).
10. As alluded to earlier, there is a vast difference between Calvin's view of the covenant and that of Martin Luther. The latter radically separated Moses and Christ, as two totally distinct covenant heads: the Old and the New. The Old Covenant is not viewed by Luther as a forerunner of the New, but its opposite. The Mosaic economy is the antithesis of the New era. This is a serious error which may explain why Luther's worldview was never as sound as that of John Calvin (Cornelis Vanderwaal, *The Covenantal Gospel,* pp. 60ff.).
11. Ronald S. Wallace, *Calvin's Doctrine of the Word and Sacrament,* pp. 27-60.

12. Westminster Confession of Faith, XIX:3.
13. Wilhelm Niesel, *The Theology of Calvin*, p. 94.
14. Westminster Confession of Faith, XXVII:1.
15. XXVII:5.

Chapter Seven: Calvin on Christ

1. "Earliest Christian Creeds," as cited in J.J. Davis, *Handbook of Basic Bible Texts*, p. 61.
2. Ronald Wallace wrongly asserts that Calvin's Christology focuses on the "functional" aspect rather than on the "essential" (or "ontological"). He further contends that this is likewise the stress of the New Testament writers themselves (*Calvin, Geneva and the Reformation*, p. 241). Here Wallace is in agreement with Oscar Cullmann (and other New Testament scholars) (*The Christology of the New Testament*, pp. 3, 4). Robert L. Reymond, however, trenchantly argues against such a notion: "I . . . insist that it is really rather superficial to suggest that men can forever concentrate on what Jesus did for them and never address the ontological question of who He is. Indeed, it is as psychologically impossible for modern men as it was for the men of New Testament times to be satisfied with an interest only in Jesus' functional significance and never question or address the ontological issue that His functional significance forces upon them" (*Jesus, Divine Messiah: The New Testament Witness*, pp. 12, 13).
3. G.C. Berkouwer, *The Person of Christ*, pp. 85-97.
4. This doctrine is sometimes referred to as the *"extra-calvinisticum"*—the Calvinistic "extra." Calvin taught that God the Son was not only incarnate in Jesus of Nazareth, but that he was also outside *(extra)* of him at the same time. As eternal Deity, the Son can in no way be restricted to a human body; he must always retain the divine attribute of omnipresence.
5. Millard Erickson, *Christian Theology*, p. 738.
6. Westminster Shorter Catechism, Q. 24.
7. Q. 25.
8. Calvin does not use the words "active" and "passive" when referring to the obedience rendered by Christ. The meaning, however, seems present (*Commentary* on Matthew 26:17; John 2:13; Hebrews 10:10).
9. Robert Peterson, *Calvin's Doctrine of the Atonement*, p. 50.
10. See R.C. Sproul, *The Glory of Christ*, p. 161.
11. Douglas Kelly, *If God Already Knows, Why Pray?* p. 39.
12. Westminster Shorter Catechism, Q. 26.
13. Robert Paul, "The Atonement: Sacrifice and Penalty," in *Readings in Calvin's Theology*, Donald K. McKim, editor, p. 145.
14. See also Ronald Wallace, *Calvin, Geneva and the Reformation*, pp.

242-252; and Robert A. Peterson, *Calvin's Doctrine of the Atonement.*
15. It is somewhat difficult to see how scholars such as Ronald Wallace (p. 251n) and Augustus H. Strong (*Systematic Theology,* pp. 777, 778) can conclude from their studies that Calvin did not hold to a "limited" or "particular" view of the atonement, *i.e.,* that Christ died to render certain the salvation of the elect, rather than making possible the salvation of all humanity ("universal" atonement). In his *Commentary* on 1 John 2:2, for example, Calvin calls the universal view of the atonement a "monstrous" doctrine which "deserves no refutation." Christ, contends Calvin, suffered "efficiently only for the elect." Gregg Singer confirms this. He writes, "An atonement which is universal is foreign to his [Calvin's] system. Christ died for the elect. A limited atonement is integral to the biblical doctrine of election, and Calvin made election pivotal in his doctrine of salvation because it occupies that place in the Scriptures" (*John Calvin: His Roots and Fruits,* p. 15).
16. See Leon Morris, *The Apostolic Preaching of the Cross,* pp. 144ff.
17. See Robert Peterson, pp. 1-10.
18. Peterson, pp. 46-54.

Chapter Eight: Calvin on Salvation
1. Calvin does not use the term *ordo salutis,* but according to Louis Berkhof he was one of the very first "to group the various parts of the order of salvation in a systematic way" (*Systematic Theology,* p. 417).
2. Westminster Shorter Catechism, Q. 87.
3. Q. 86.
4. Q. 33.
5. See John Gerstner, *Handout Theology,* p. 48; and Francois Wendel, "Justification and Predestination in Calvin," *Readings in Calvin's Theology,* Donald K. McKim, editor, p. 153.
6. Cited by Wendel, p. 156.
7. Gerstner, pp. 48, 49.
8. Westminster Shorter Catechism, Q. 35.
9. Ronald Wallace, *Calvin, Geneva and the Reformation,* pp. 210-214.
10. Cited by Wendel, p. 173.

Chapter Nine: Calvin on the Church
1. "A Brief Explanation of the Ten Commandments, the Creed, and the Lord's Prayer," cited in *Handbook of Basic Bible Texts,* J.J. Davis, p. 103.
2. Louis Berkhof, *Systematic Theology,* pp. 560-578; Berkhof lists only the first three of the attributes. See *Institutes* IV:1-19.
3. From the *Corpus Reformatorum,* cited in Wilhelm Niesel, *The Theology of*

Calvin, p. 209.

4. Ronald Wallace, *Calvin's Doctrine of the Word and Sacrament,* pp. 99, 100.

5. G.S.M. Walker, "Calvin and the Church," *Readings in Calvin's Theology,* Donald K. McKim, p. 229; Ronald Wallace, *Calvin, Geneva and the Reformation,* p. 21. Although it has been claimed that Calvin held to exclusive Psalmody in public worship, such is not the case. Calvin preferred Psalms, but he had the congregation singing other songs as well, such as a version of the Ten Commandments, the Creed, and the Lord's Prayer (G.I. Williamson, *The Scriptural Regulative Principle of Worship,* p. 17; Rowland Ward, *Psalm-Singing in Scripture and History,* pp. 28-30). At the same time, Calvin was, however, opposed to the use of musical instruments in the worship service. In his *Commentary* on Psalm 81:1-3, he writes, "With respect to the tabret, harp, and psaltery, we have formerly observed, and will find it necessary afterwards to repeat the same remark, that the Levites, under the law, were justified in making use of instrumental music in the worship of God; it having been His will to train His people, while they were as yet tender and like children by such rudiments, until the coming of Christ. But now when the clear light of the gospel has dissipated the shadows of the law, and taught us that God is served in a simpler form, it would be a foolish and mistaken part to imitate that which the prophet enjoined only upon those of his own time."

6. F. Nigel Lee, *The Covenantal Sabbath,* pp. 255, 256.

7. Louis Berkhof, p. 570.

8. Wallace, pp. 84-87.

9. *Calvin: Theological Treatises,* J.K.S. Reid, editor, pp. 29, 30.

10. Westminster Confession of Faith, XXVII:1; Westminster Shorter Catechism, Q. 92.

11. G.R. Potter and M. Greengrass, *John Calvin,* pp. 34, 35.

12. Westminster Confession of Faith, XXVII:13.

13. Wallace, pp. 159ff.

14. *Draft Ecclesiastical Ordinances* (1541), cited in Potter and Greengrass, p. 74; see also Calvin's *Commentary* on Acts 6:1ff.

15. Walker, p. 228; *Institutes* IV:3:9.

Chapter Ten: Calvin on the Last Things

1. See David E. Holwerda, "Eschatology and History," *Readings in Calvin's Theology,* Donald K. McKim, editor, pp. 311-314.

2. Ronald Wallace, *Calvin's Doctrine of the Christian Life,* p. 266.

3. Westminster Confession of Faith, XXXII, 2.

4. XXXII:3.

5. Wallace, pp. 79, 80; Ian Murray, *The Puritan Hope,* p. 40.

6. Westminster Confession of Faith, XXV:6; 1647 edition.
7. XXXIII:3.

APPENDIX

The Five Points of Calvinism

It should be obvious to any reader that Calvin taught a complete system of theology, much more than five points. Yet the phrase, "the five points of Calvinism," is better known than either Calvin's system of theology or the five points themselves. Perhaps one of the reasons is the acronym, TULIP, by which the five points have been summarized:

Total depravity
Unconditional election
Limited atonement
Irresistible grace
Perseverance of the saints.

In the late sixteenth and early seventeenth century a professor of theology at the University of Leiden in the Netherlands, James Arminius, began teaching ideas that contradicted the doctrine of the Reformers. Arminius disagreed with Calvin on the nature of man, the sovereignty of God, the effectiveness of Christ's work, the power of God, and the Christian life.

In 1610, a year after Arminius died, his followers wrote

five points of doctrine and asked the government of Holland to amend the Belgic Confession of Faith and the Heidelberg Catechism (the official statements of faith of the churches in Holland). These five points may be summarized as follows:

1. God elects and reproves on the basis of foreseen faith or disbelief.
2. Christ died for each and every man, but only believers are saved.
3. Divine grace is necessary for faith or any good deed.
4. This grace may be resisted.
5. Whether all who are regenerated by God will persevere in the faith is a point that needs further investigation.

From November 1618 to May 1619 a meeting of many Protestant churches of Europe was held in the city of Dordrecht in the Netherlands to examine the teachings of Arminius and his followers. This Synod of Dort rejected the teachings of Arminius as unbiblical and wrote five chapters against them; these chapters became known as the five points of Calvinism.

These five points, although they are far from a complete statement of Calvinism, do form a logical system. One point both implies and requires the other four; to deny one is to be both Scripturally unsound and logically inconsistent.

A few of the many Bible verses supporting the five points of Calvinism follow:

The Total Depravity of Man

All men are ethically dead, not sick or disabled. They cannot do, think, or believe good.

There is none righteous, no, not one; there is none who understands; there is none who seeks after God. They have all gone out of the way; they have together become unprofitable; there is none who does good, no, not one. Their throat is an open tomb; with their tongues they have practiced deceit; the poison of asps is under their lips, whose mouth is full of cursing and bitterness. Their feet are swift to shed blood; destruction and misery are in their ways; and the way of peace they have not known. There is no fear of God before their eyes. . . . All have sinned and fall short of the glory of God.

Romans 3:10-18, 23.

And the Lord God commanded the man, saying, "Of every tree of the garden you may freely eat; but of the tree of the knowledge of good and evil you shall not eat, for in the day that you eat of it you shall surely die."

Genesis 2:16-17.

Then the Lord saw that the wickedness of man was great in the earth, and that every intent of the thoughts of his heart was only evil continually.

Genesis 6:5.

The heart is deceitful above all things, and desperately wicked; who can know it?

Jeremiah 17:9.

For from within, out of the heart of men, proceed evil thoughts, adulteries, fornications, murders, thefts, covetousness, wickedness, deceit, licentiousness, an evil eye, blasphemy, pride, foolishness. All these evil things come from within and defile a man.

Mark 7:21-23.

For to be carnally minded is death, but to be spiritually minded is life and peace, because the carnal mind is enmity against God. It is not subject to the law of God, nor indeed can be. So then, those who are in the flesh cannot please God.

Romans 8:6-8.

But the natural man does not receive the things of the Spirit of God, for they are foolishness to him; nor can he know them, because they are spiritually discerned.

1 Corinthians 2:14.

Therefore, just as through one man sin entered the world, and death through sin, and thus death spread to all men because all sinned.

Romans 5:12.

And you he made alive, who were dead in trespasses and sins, in which you once walked, according to the course of this world, according to the prince of the power of the air, the spirit who now works in the sons of disobedience, among whom also we all once conducted ourselves in the lusts of our flesh, fulfilling the desires of the flesh and of the mind, and were by nature children of wrath, just as the others.

Ephesians 2:1-3.

And a servant of the Lord must not quarrel but be gentle to all, able to teach, patient, in humility correcting those who are in opposition, if God perhaps will grant them repentance, so that they may know the truth, and that they may come to their senses and escape the snare of the devil, having been taken captive by him to do his will.

2 Timothy 2:24-26.

Do not enter into judgment with your servant, for in your sight no one living is righteous.

Psalm 143:2.

All we like sheep have gone astray; we have turned, every one, to his own way; and the Lord has laid on him the iniquity of us all.

Isaiah 53:6.

No one can come to me unless the Father who sent me draws him. . . .

John 6:44.

Behold, I was brought forth in iniquity, and in sin my mother conceived me.

Psalm 51:5.

The Unconditional Election of God the Father

Since men are not good at all, God chooses those whom he wishes to save completely out of his mercy and grace.

For the children not yet being born, nor having done any good or evil, that the purpose of God according to election might stand, not of works but of him who calls. . . . As it is written, Jacob I have loved but Esau I have hated. . . . I will have mercy on whomever I will have mercy, and I will have compassion on whomever I will have compassion. So then it is not of him who wills, nor of him who runs, but of God who shows mercy. . . . Therefore he has mercy on whom he wills, and whom he wills he hardens. . . . Does not the potter have power over the clay, from the same lump to make one vessel for honor and another for dishonor? What if God, wanting to show his wrath and to make his power known, endured with much longsuffering the vessels of wrath prepared for destruction, that he might make known the riches of his glory on the vessels of mercy, which he had prepared beforehand for glory?

Romans 9:11-13, 15-16, 18, 21-23.

Behold the nations are as a drop in a bucket, and are counted as the small dust on the balance. Look, he lifts up the isles as a very little thing, and Lebanon is not sufficient to burn, nor its beasts sufficient for a burnt offering. All nations before him are as nothing. And they are counted by him less than nothing and worthless. . . . It is he who sits above the circle of the earth, and its inhabitants are like grasshoppers, who stretches out the heavens like a curtain, and spreads them out like a tent to dwell in. He brings the princes to nothing; he makes the judges of the earth useless. . . . He gives power to the weak, and to those who have no might he increases strength. Even the youths shall faint and be weary, and their young men shall utterly fall, but those who wait on the Lord shall renew their strength; they shall mount up with wings like eagles, they shall run and not be weary, they shall walk and not faint.

Isaiah 40:15-17, 22-23, 29-31.

Blessed is the man whom you choose and cause to approach you.

Psalm 65:4.

All things have been delivered to me by my father, and no one knows the Son except the Father. Nor does anyone know the Father except the Son, and he to whom the Sons wills to reveal him.

Matthew 11:27.

And we know that all things work together for good to those who love God, to those who are called according to his purpose. For whom he foreknew, he also predestined to be conformed to the image of his Son, that he might be the firstborn among many brethren. Moreover, whom he predestined, these he also called; whom he called, these he also justified; and whom he justified, these he also glorified.

Romans 8:28-30.

But you are a chosen generation, a royal priesthood, a holy nation, his own special people, that you may proclaim the praises of him who called you out of darkness into his marvelous light; who once were not a people but are now the people of God, who had not obtained mercy but now have obtained mercy.

1 Peter 2:9-10.

And unless the Lord had shortened those days, no flesh

would be saved; but for the elect's sake, whom he chose, he shortened the days.

Mark 13:20.

Blessed be the God and Father of our Lord Jesus Christ, who has blessed us with every spiritual blessing in the heavenly places in Christ, just as he chose us in him before the foundation of the world, that we should be holy and without blame before him in love, having predestined us to adoption as sons by Jesus Christ to himself, according to the good pleasure of his will, to the praise of the glory of his grace, by which he has made us accepted in the beloved.

Ephesians 1:3-4.

But God has chosen the foolish things of the world to put to shame the wise, and God has chosen the weak things of the world to put to shame the things which are mighty; and the base things of the world and the things which are despised God has chosen, and the things which are not, to bring to nothing the things that are, that no flesh should glory in his presence.

1 Corinthians 1:27-29.

Who has saved us and called us with a holy calling, not according to our works, but according to his own purpose and grace which was given to us in Christ Jesus before time began.

2 Timothy 1:9.

But to as many as received him, to them he gave the right to become children of God, even to those who believe in his name: who were born, not of blood, nor of the will of the flesh, nor of the will of man, but of God.

John 1:12-13.

All the inhabitants of the earth are reputed as nothing; he does according to his will in the army of heaven and among the inhabitants of the earth. No one can restrain his hand or say to him, "What have you done?"

Daniel 4:35.

The Limited Atonement of Christ

Christ actually saves those, and only those, whom God has chosen to be saved.

And she will bring forth a son, and you shall call his name Jesus, for he will save his people from their sins.
Matthew 1:21.

Jesus spoke these words, lifted up his eyes to heaven, and said: "Father, the hour has come. Glorify your son, that your son also may glorify you, as you have given him authority over all flesh, that he should give eternal life to as many as you have given him. And this is eternal life, that they may know you, the only true God, and Jesus Christ whom you have sent.

"I have glorified you on earth. I have finished the work which you have given me to do. . . . I have manifested your name to the men whom you have given me out of the world. They were yours, you gave them to me, and they have kept your word. Now they have known that all things which you have given me are from you. For I have given to them the words which you have given me; and they have received them, and have known surely that I came forth from you; and they have believed that you sent me.

"I pray for them. I do not pray for the world, but for those whom you have given me, for they are yours. And all mine are yours, and yours are mine, and I am glorified in them.

"Now I am no longer in the world, but these are in the world, and I come to you. Holy Father, keep through your name those whom you have given me, that they may be one as we are. . . . I do not pray for these alone, but also for those who will believe in me through their word. . . ."
John 17:1-11, 20.

And Jesus said to them, "I am the bread of life. He who comes to me shall never hunger, and he who believes in me shall never thirst. But I said to you that you have seen me and yet do not believe. All that the Father gives me will come to me, and the one who comes to me I will by no means cast out. For I have come down from heaven, not to do my own will, but the will of him who sent me. This is the will of the Father who sent me, that of all he has given me I should lose nothing, but should raise it up at the last day."

John 6:35-39.

"I am the good shepherd. The good shepherd gives his life for the sheep. . . . I am the good shepherd; and I know my sheep, and am known by my own. As the Father knows me, even do I know the Father; and I lay down my life for the sheep."

John 10:11, 14.

Then the Jews surrounded him and said to him, "How long do you keep us in doubt? If you are the Christ, tell us plainly."

Jesus answered them, "I told you, and you do not believe. The works that I do in my Father's name, they bear witness of me. But you do not believe, because you are not of my sheep, as I said to you. My sheep hear my voice, and I know them, and they follow me. And I give them eternal life, and they shall never perish; neither shall anyone snatch them out of my hand."

John 10:24-28.

And he said, "To you it has been given to know the mysteries of the kingdom of God, but to the rest it is given in parables, that seeing they may not see, and hearing they may not understand."

Luke 8:10.

The Irresistible Grace of the Holy Spirit

Man cannot resist God, who is all powerful.

"For as the Father raises the dead and gives life to them, even so the Son gives life to whom he will."

John 5:21.

And as many as had been appointed unto eternal life believed.

Acts 13:48.

"My word shall not return to me void, but it shall accomplish what I please, and it shall prosper in the thing for which I sent it."

Isaiah 55:11.

"I will have mercy on whomever I will have mercy, and I will have compassion on whomever I will have compassion." So then it is not of him who wills, nor of him who runs, but of God who shows mercy. . . . Therefore he has mercy on whom he wills, and whom he wills he hardens. . . . Does not the potter have power over the clay, from the same lump to make one vessel for honor and another for dishonor? What if God, wanting to show his wrath and to make his power known, endured with much longsuffering the vessels of wrath prepared for destruction, that he might make known the riches of his glory on the vessels of mercy, which he had prepared beforehand for glory?

Romans 9:15-16, 18, 21-23.

The Perseverance of the Saints

God, who is omnipotent, will not permit anyone for whom Christ died to be lost.

But now thus says the Lord who created you, O Jacob, and he who formed you, O Israel: "Fear not, for I have redeemed

you; I have called you by your name; you are mine. When you pass through the waters, I will be with you; and through the rivers, they shall not overflow you. When you walk through the fire, you shall not be burned, nor shall the flame scorch you. For I am the Lord your God, the Holy One of Israel, your Saviour."
Isaiah 43:1-3.

"What do you think? If a man has a hundred sheep, and one of them goes astray, does he not leave the ninety-nine and go to the mountains to seek the one that is straying? And if he should find it, assuredly, I say to you, he rejoices more over that sheep than over the ninety-nine that did not go astray. Even so it is not the will of your Father who is in heaven that one of these little ones should perish."
Matthew 18:12-14.

"For God so loved the world that he gave his only begotten son, that whoever believes in him should not perish but have everlasting life."
John 3:16.

"Most assuredly, I say to you, he who hears my word and believes in him who sent me has everlasting life, and shall not come into judgment, but has passed from death to life."
John 5:24.

"My sheep hear my voice, and I know them, and they follow me. And I give them eternal life, and they shall never perish; neither shall anyone snatch them out of my hand."
John 10:27-28.

But God demonstrates his own love toward us, in that while we were still sinners, Christ died for us. Much more then, having now been justified by his blood, we shall be saved from wrath through him. For if when we were enemies we were reconciled to God through the death of his Son, much more, having been reconciled, we shall be saved by his life.
Romans 5:8-10.

Who shall separate us from the love of Christ? Shall tribulation, or distress, or persecution, or famine, or nakedness, or peril, or sword? As it is written, "For your sake we are killed all day long; we are accounted as sheep for the slaughter." Yet in all these things we are more than conquerors through him who loved us. For I am persuaded that neither death not life, nor angels nor principalities nor powers, nor things present nor things to come, nor height nor depth, nor any other created thing shall be able to separate us from the love of God which is in Christ Jesus our Lord.

Romans 8:35-39.

Who will also confirm you to the end, that you may be blameless in the day of our Lord Jesus Christ. God is faithful, by whom you were called into the fellowship of his Son, Jesus Christ our Lord.

1 Corinthians 1:8-9.

Now may the God of peace himself sanctify you completely; and may your whole spirit, soul, and body be preserved blameless at the coming of our Lord Jesus Christ. He who calls you is faithful, who also will do it.

1 Thessalonians 5:23-24.

Blessed be the God and Father of our Lord Jesus Christ, who according to his abundant mercy has begotten us again to a living hope through the resurrection of Jesus Christ from the dead, to an inheritance incorruptible and undefiled and that does not fade away, reserved in heaven for you, who are kept by the power of God through faith for salvation ready to be revealed in the last time.

1 Peter 1:3-5.

John W. Robbins

GLOSSARY

Abrogate: to abolish or nullify a (biblical) law.

Adoption: that act of God by which he brings justified sinners into a filial relationship with himself.

Amanuensis: one who functions as a secretary.

Amillennialism: the eschatological view that there will be no age of gospel prosperity and blessings on earth that will see Christianity as the predominant "religion" or world view. Christ's second advent will be followed by a general resurrection and judgment.

Anabaptists: that radical wing of the Protestant Reformation which adhered to a number of unorthodox doctrines, one of which was that because the sacrament of baptism was only for believers, all babies baptized in infancy needed to be rebaptized (thus the name "Anabaptist"). Other such unorthodox doctrines included soul sleep, pacifism, that absolute (or nearly absolute) purity within the church of Jesus Christ could be brought about through proper church discipline, the right to disobey any civil government that did not strictly adhere to biblical law, and faith itself as being a "good work." There were various sects within this movement, each adopting its own idiosyncratic doctrines.

Annihilationism: the teaching that some human souls (*i.e.,* unbelievers), if not all, will cease to exist after death; they are to be annihilated.

Anselm (1033-1109): a medieval philosopher and theologian who is best known for his formulation of the ontological argument for God's existence, *i.e.,* God is "that than which nothing greater can be conceived."

129

Anthropology: the study of man.

Antinomianism: the theological view that no one is obligated to obey the moral law.

Apologetics: the discipline which concerns itself with the philosophical defense of the Christian faith and world view.

A posteriori: term designating a kind of knowledge which can only be gained by experience, observation, or experiment; it is knowledge formulated "after experience."

A priori: term designating a kind of knowledge which is "before experience"; innate, intuitive, or revealed.

Aristocracy: that form of government where the rule is in the hands of the "best" or privileged citizens. In Calvin's day it was a form of republican government.

Aristotle (384-322): a Greek philosopher, student of Plato, and tutor of Alexander the Great. An empiricist, Aristotle later founded his own school, the Lyceum.

Asceticism: that religious movement which stresses a life of austere self-discipline.

Assurance: that gracious work of God wherein he brings justified sinners into a state of grace in which they can be assured of their salvation.

Atonement: the biblical teaching concerning the reconciliation of God and man (making "at-one-ment"), through the redemptive life, death, and resurrection of Jesus Christ.

Augustine, Aurelius (354-430): bishop of Hippo (North Africa). Perhaps the greatest theologian and philosopher of the early church.

Axiom: an indemonstrable first principle or truth.

Barth, Karl (1886-1968): a Swiss scholar; one of the most influential neo-orthodox theologians of the 20th century.

Basil the Great (c. 330-379): an early bishop of Caesarea and defender of orthodox doctrine.

Bibliology: the study of the doctrine of revelation, particularly special revelation.

Brunner, Heinrich Emil (1889-1966): a highly influential Swiss neo-orthodox theologian.

Bucer, Martin (1491-1551): a leading figure in the Protestant Reformation; he greatly influenced John Calvin.

Canon: the 66 books of the Old and New Testaments, in which God's special revelation is communicated to mankind by his Spirit.

Christology: the study of the doctrine of Jesus Christ.

Chrysostom, John (c. 347-407): one of the early teachers of the Greek church; the name Chrysostom means "golden-mouthed."

Conditional immortality: the teaching that the souls of unbelievers sink into nothingness at death, but God imparts to the redeemed the gift of immortality.

Consubstantiation: the teaching of Lutheranism that Christ's body and blood are physically "contained" in the elements at the Lord's Supper; that is, they are in, with, and under the bread and wine.

Conversion: the gracious act of God by which he causes regenerated persons to respond to the effectual call. It consists of both repentance and saving faith.

Cosmological argument: the so-called "theistic proof" for God that proceeds from effect to cause. The universe is an effect, so the argument goes, which needs a cause: God.

Covenant: a binding agreement between two or more parties. In the Bible, such covenants are (usually) between God and his creatures.

Covenant of grace: the covenant, first suggested in Genesis 3:15, in which God covenanted with the elect sinners, represented by Christ, to apply the benefits of salvation to them, each and every one. They, on the other hand, covenant to put their full faith and trust in Christ, as their Savior and Lord.

Covenant of works: the original covenant which God made with Adam as the federal head of the entire human race, in which he promised him, and his progeny, manifold blessings, including eternal life. The condition of the covenant was that Adam perfectly obey God's commandments. The penalty for disobedience was death, both physical and spiritual (Genesis 2:6,17).

Covenant theology: the system of theology which maintains that all of the post-fall covenants are essentially one; they are all part and parcel of the one covenant of grace.

Creationism: the theory that the body of man is propagated by the parents, but the spirit, or non-physical element, is an immediate creation of God.

Decree: God's eternal purpose by which he has sovereignly and unchangeably foreordained all things which will ever happen. Technically speaking, there is only one eternal purpose of God, but because there are many secondary purposes, it is frequently referred to in the plural (decrees).

Decretive will: God's purposes; it is absolute and determined by him alone. Unlike the preceptive will of God, it is not for man to know, unless God reveals it.

Deism: belief in the existence of God as the creator of the universe, who after the completion of creation exerts no continual influence over his creation.

Descartes, Rene (1596-1650): a French philosopher of the rationalist school, sometimes referred to as the father of modern philosophy.

Determinism: the belief that there are no contingent events. All things are necessarily determined by antecedent causes.

Dichotomy: used in discussing the biblical teaching that man is a "living soul" consisting of a physical body and a non-physical spirit (Genesis 2:7).

Dispensationalism: the system of theology which holds that the various biblical covenants are to be viewed as periods of time (dispensations) in which God alters his relationship with mankind.

Ecclesiology: the study of the doctrine of the church.

Economy: a theological term referring to an administrative order or function.

Effectual call: the work of the Holy Spirit, by which he applies the external call of the gospel to the heart of the elect sinner.

Election: God's sovereign and eternal decree to save some men, in and through the person and work of Jesus Christ.

Eschatology: the study of the doctrine of the "last things," both individual and general.

Evidentialism: the system of apologetics which holds that Christians should attempt to prove the existence of God and his infallible Word from a series of "theistic proofs," based on sense experience (empiricism). It argues from sensory evidence to God and his Word.

Exegesis: detailed analysis and explanation or interpretation of a text.

External or universal call: that general call of the gospel to all who come under the preaching of the Word, by which God commands all men to repent, even those whom he has predestinated unto eternal death.

Faith: "saving faith" is that saving grace by which the elect sinner understands and believes the Word of God.

Fatalism: the belief that one's fate is predetermined, regardless of one's actions.

Federal headship: the doctrine that one person stands as the representative of many. Adam is the federal head of the entire human race under the covenant of works. Christ is the federal head of the elect under the covenant of grace.

Foreknowledge: God's knowledge of all things before they happen.

Foreordination: God's sovereign and eternal decree concerning all of his creation.

General revelation: the innate knowledge of God which he has given to all mankind.

Glorification: the final state of salvation, by which the elect pass into the very presence of God at their death.

Gospel: the good news that Jesus Christ died for the sins of his people, that he was buried, and on the third day was raised from the dead, according to the Scriptures (1 Corinthians 15:3,4).

Hermeneutics: the science and methodology of biblical interpretation.

Imputation: the act of ascribing something to another.

Inerrancy: the teaching that the Scriptures are free from all error.

Infallibility: the teaching that the Bible is without defect in every sense of the word; it is absolutely unimpeachable; it cannot err. Further, it always accomplishes that which God intends it to accomplish.

Infralapsarianism: the view concerning the logical order of the decrees of God which maintains that God decreed to permit the fall prior to his decree to elect some and damn others.

Innate knowledge: that knowledge which is inborn.

Inspiration: the immediate influence of God with regard to the writing of Scripture by which he so controlled the authors that their writings were infallible and inerrant. The Scriptures are the actual product of God's "breath"; they are his creative work; they are the very Word of God.

Invisible church: the "true" church of Jesus Christ; the elect of God, of both the Old and New Testaments. These are "invisible" to mankind, who can never search the hearts of others, but they are not invisible to God.

Justification: that act of God by which he declares elect sinners to be innocent and righteous, based on the perfect righteousness of Jesus Christ which is imputed to them.

Justin Martyr (c. 105-165): one of the earliest and most important Christian apologists. He was martyred for his faith.

Knox, John (1514-1572): a Scottish Reformer who was heavily influenced by John Calvin and the principle of *sola scriptura.*

Logos: a Greek word meaning "word," "logic," "reason," "ratio." Christ is the Word *(Logos)* of God (John 1:1).

Means of grace: those means by which the Spirit of God ministers to the saints (the Scriptures together with the Sacraments and prayer), building them up in the faith.

Melanchthon, Philip (1497-1560): a German theologian and close associate of Martin Luther.

Modalism: the doctrine that God is one in essence and one in person. There are not three persons within the Godhead, there are merely three modes (Father, Son, Holy Spirit) in which one person functions.

Natural theology: that theory of evidentialist apologetics that maintains that not only is there a true general revelation which God gives to mankind, but also that it is possible for man to express true knowledge of God from this general revelation alone (*i.e.,* without the aid of special revelation).

Ordo salutis: a Latin phrase which refers to the logical order in which salvation is applied to the elect.

Orthodoxy: the traditional views of the Christian faith as expressed in the creeds of the church.

Paradox: a contradictory or seemingly contradictory statement.

Perseverance: that saving grace of God by which he so works in the life of the justified sinner that he will persevere to the end and be saved.

Plato (428-348): a Greek philosopher who studied under Socrates. A rationalist, he founded his own school, the Academy, where he taught until his death.

Plenary inspiration: that view of inspiration which maintains that all 66 books of the Bible are equally inspired.

Pneumatology: the study of the doctrine of the Holy Spirit.

Postmillennialism: the eschatological view that Christ will return after (post) the millennium. Prior to his return, the gospel will eventually so permeate the nations, that they will be predominantly "Christianized." This period of gospel prosperity will bring about visible, worldwide blessings in all areas of life, economic as well as spiritual.

Preceptive will: God's commands which are revealed in Scripture.

Predestination: God's sovereign and eternal purposes concerning his moral creatures, *i.e.,* mankind, both with regard to the election of some and the reprobation of others.

Premillennialism: the eschatological view that Christ will return before (pre) the millennium, to resurrect the saints and establish his worldwide rule—both politically and spiritually. This thousand year period will bring peace and prosperity.

Presbyterianism: the biblical form of church government which adheres to the principle of "rule by elders (presbyters)."

Presuppositionalism: the system of apologetics which avers that the existence of God and the infallibility of his Word are to be presupposed (assumed) as indemonstrable axioms; they cannot be proved; they are the ground of all proof. It argues from Scripture, not to God and Scripture.

Propitiation: the removal or taking away of the sins of the elect, by the atoning work of Jesus Christ, in which the wrath of God is appeased.

Providence: the sovereign work of God whereby he governs, sustains, and preserves all his creatures and achieves all his eternal purposes.

Regeneration: the work of the Holy Spirit, by which he prepares the heart of the elect sinner to respond to the effectual call of God. When an individual is regenerated, he is "born again."

Reincarnation: the teaching that the soul, after death, becomes incarnate in a succession of bodies, as it undergoes purification.

Repentance: that saving grace wherein elect sinners abhor and turn from their sin unto Jesus Christ, trusting in him alone for their salvation. It is, literally, a "change of mind" with regard to sin and God.

Reprobation: God's sovereign and eternal decree to condemn some men to hell.

Sacraments: the two New Testament signs and seals of the covenant of grace, baptism and the Lord's Supper.

Sanctification: that gracious work of God by which elect sinners are enabled progressively to die to sin and to live to righteousness. It is the "Christianizing of the Christian."

Self-authenticating: that which is proved or established as authentic in and of itself. Calvin maintained that Scripture was self-authenticating and self-evident; it proved itself to be the very Word of God.

Seneca (3-65): a Roman philosopher who was the chief figure of "Stoicism" during his later years. He was a tutor of Nero, and became his Consul and his victim during Nero's reign as emperor.

Session: that body of ruling and teaching elders, elected by the congregation, who rule over a local church, under Christ, in accordance with his Word.

Sola scriptura: a Latin phrase meaning "Scripture alone." This Reformation principle maintains that God's Word is fully adequate to equip us "for every good work," *i.e.,* for all matters of faith and life (2 Timothy 3:16,17).

Soteriology: the study of the doctrine of salvation.

Soul sleep: the false teaching which maintains that the soul sleeps between death and the resurrection.

Special revelation: God's verbal (and redemptive) self-revelation, which was given to mankind over a period of some 1500 years, until the canon of Scripture was finally closed with the New Testament. Today, special revelation is communicated to us only through the Bible.

Spurgeon, Charles Haddon (1834-1892): an influential Baptist minister in England, who strongly endorsed Calvinism.

Stoicism: a materialist school of Greek philosophy which held that the world, including mankind, is rationally determined by the universal *logos* (reason).

Subordinationism: the doctrine that there is one God who is the Father. The Son and the Spirit are lesser gods, if gods at all.

Supralapsarianism: the view concerning the logical order of the decrees of God which maintains that God decreed to save a certain number of men (the elect) and condemn others (the reprobate), prior to his decree to permit the fall.

Tertullian (c. 155-220): an early Latin theologian and apologist. He first coined the term "Trinity." Later in his life he became an ascetic.

Theism: belief in the existence of God, or a god, or gods.

Theology: the study of the doctrine of God.

Total depravity: the teaching that because of the fall of Adam, man, in and of himself, is unable to please God. He is spiritually dead.

Traducianism: the theory that both the physical bodies and non-physical spirits of men are propagated by their parents.

Transubstantiation: the teaching of Roman Catholicism that the bread and wine at the Mass are miraculously transformed into Christ's body and blood.

Trichotomy: the teaching that the nature of man is threefold: body, soul, and spirit.

Turretin, Francis (1623-1687): an Italian Calvinist theologian who ministered in Geneva most of his life.

Verbal inspiration: that view of inspiration which maintains that the very words, not just the ideas, of Scripture are "God-breathed."

Visible church: all of those who make a public profession of Jesus Christ, along with their covenant children.

Warfield, Benjamin B. (1851-1921): one of the last of a line of conservative theologians who taught at Princeton Seminary; a staunch defender of Calvinism.

Weltanschauung: a German term referring to one's "world view," *i.e.,* the way one views all of life.

BIBLIOGRAPHY

Alexander, J.H., *Ladies of the Reformation*. England: Gospel Standard Strict Baptist Trust, 1978.

Berkhof, Louis, *Systematic Theology*. Grand Rapids: Eerdmans, 1941 [1939].

Berkouwer, G.C., *Man: The Image of God*. Grand Rapids: Eerdmans, 1962.

Berkouwer, G.C., *The Person of Christ*. Grand Rapids: Eerdmans, 1954.

Beveridge, Henry, and Bonnet, Jules, editors, *Selected Works of John Calvin*. Vols. 1-7, Grand Rapids: Baker, 1983.

Bogue, Carl W., *The Genesis Covenants*. Akron: Faith Presbyterian Church, 1986.

Calvin, John, *Commentaries*. Vols. I-XXII, Grand Rapids: Baker, 1981.

Calvin, John, *Institutes of the Christian Religion*. Vols. I & II, Library of the Christian Classics, John T. McNeill, editor, translated by Ford Lewis Battles, Philadelphia: Westminster, 1960.

Calvin, John, *Sermons on Deuteronomy*. Edinburgh: Banner of Truth, 1987.

Calvin, John, *Sermons on Ephesians*. Edinburgh: Banner of Truth, 1973.

Calvin, John, *Sermons on Timothy and Titus*. Edinburgh: Banner of Truth, 1983.

Clark, Gordon H., *The Atonement*. Jefferson: The Trinity Foundation, 1987.

Clark, Gordon H., *The Concept of Biblical Authority*. Phillipsburg: Presbyterian and Reformed, 1979.

Cullman, Oscar, *The Christology of the New Testament*. Philadelphia: Westminster, 1963.

Davis, John Jefferson, *Handbook of Basic Bible Texts*. Grand Rapids: Zondervan, 1984.

Dillenberger, John, editor, *John Calvin: Selections from His Writings*. Missoula: Scholars Press, 1975.

Elwell, Walter A., editor, *Evangelical Dictionary of Theology*. Grand Rapids: Baker, 1984.

139

Erickson, Millard J., *Christian Theology.* Grand Rapids: Baker, 1983, 1984, 1985.

Ferguson, Sinclair B., *John Owen on the Christian Life.* Edinburgh: Banner of Truth, 1987.

Ferguson, Sinclair B., David F. Wright, and J.I. Packer, editors, *New Dictionary of Theology.* Downers Grove: Inter Varsity, 1988.

Gerstner, John H., *Handout Church History.* Orlando: Ligonier Ministries, 1989.

Gerstner, John H., *Handout Theology.* Orlando: Ligonier Ministries, 1989.

Gerstner, John H., *Jonathan Edwards: A Mini-Theology.* Wheaton: Tyndale, 1987.

Gerstner, John H., *The Rational Biblical Theology of Jonathan Edwards.* Vol. I, Powhatan: Berea, and Orlando: Ligonier, 1991.

Haroutunian, Joseph, translator and editor, *Calvin: Commentaries.* Philadelphia: Westminster, 1958.

Ingram, Robert F., editor, *Table Talk.* Orlando: Ligonier, 1991.

Kelly, Douglas F., *If God Already Knows, Why Pray?* Brentwood: Wolgemuth & Hyatt, 1989.

Kerr, Hugh T., editor, *Calvin's Institutes: A New Compend.* Louisville: Westminster/John Knox, 1989.

Lee, F. Nigel, *The Covenantal Sabbath.* London: Lord's Day Observance Society, 1970.

Lee, F. Nigel, *John Calvin: True Presbyterian.* Wavell Heights: Jesus Lives, 1981.

McKim, Donald K., editor, *Readings in Calvin's Theology.* Grand Rapids: Baker, 1984.

Morris, Leon, *The Apostolic Preaching of the Cross.* Grand Rapids: Eerdmans, 1965.

Murray, Iain, *The Puritan Hope.* Edinburgh: Banner of Truth, 1971.

Murray, John, *Calvin on Scripture and Divine Sovereignty.* Hertfordshire: Evangelical Press, 1979.

Murray, John, *Collected Writings.* Vols. I-IV, Edinburgh: Banner of Truth, 1976.

Nash, Ronald H., *The Word of God and the Mind of Man.* Grand Rapids: Zondervan, 1982.

Niesel, Wilhelm, *The Theology of Calvin.* translated by Harold Knight, Philadelphia: Westminster, 1956.

Packer, J.I., *A Quest for Godliness.* Wheaton: Crossway, 1990.

Peterson, Robert A., *Calvin's Doctrine of the Atonement.* Phillipsburg: Presbyterian and Reformed, 1983.

Potter, G.R., and M. Greengrass, *John Calvin.* New York: St. Martins, 1983.

Reid, J.K.S., translator and editor, *Calvin: Theological Treatises.* Philadelphia: Westminster, 1954.

Reymond, Robert L., *God and Man in Holy Scripture.* St. Louis: unpublished syllabus, Covenant Theological Seminary, 1990.

Reymond, Robert L., *Introductory Studies in Contemporary Theology.* Philadelphia: Presbyterian and Reformed, 1968.

Reymond, Robert L., *Jesus, Divine Messiah: The New Testament Witness.* Phillipsburg: Presbyterian and Reformed, 1990.

Roberts, Frank C., *To All Generations: A Study of Church History.* Grand Rapids: Bible Way, 1981.

Rushdoony, Rousas J., *By What Standard?* Nutley: Presbyterian and Reformed, 1959.

Rushdoony, Rousas J., *Politics of Guilt and Pity.* Fairfax: Thoburn Press, 1970.

Ryken, Leland, *Worldly Saints: The Puritans as They Really Were.* Grand Rapids: Zondervan, 1986.

Schaff, Philip, *History of the Christian Church.* Vols. I-VIII, Grand Rapids: Eerdmans, 1910.

Singer, C. Gregg, *John Calvin: His Roots and Fruits.* Greenville: A Press, 1989.

Sproul, R.C., *The Glory of Christ.* Wheaton: Tyndale, 1990.

Sproul, R.C., *Pleasing God.* Wheaton: Tyndale, 1988.

Sproul, R.C., John H. Gerstner, and Arthur Lindsley, *Classical Apologetics.* Grand Rapids: Zondervan, 1984.

Strong, Augustus H., *Systematic Theology.* Valley Forge: Judson, 1907.

Vanderwaal, Cornelis, *The Covenantal Gospel.* Alberta: Inheritance, 1990.

Van Til, Cornelius, *The Defense of the Faith.* Phillipsburg: Presbyterian and Reformed, 1980 [1956].

Wallace, Ronald S., *Calvin's Doctrine of the Christian Life.* Tyler: Geneva Divinity School, 1982 [1959].

Wallace, Ronald S., *Calvin's Doctrine of the Word and Sacrament.* Tyler: Geneva Divinity School, 1982 [1953].

Wallace, Ronald S., *Calvin, Geneva and the Reformation.* Grand Rapids: Baker, 1988, 1990.

Ward, Rowland, *Psalm-Singing in Scripture and History.* Melbourne: R.S. Ward, 1985.

Warfield, Benjamin B., *Biblical and Theological Studies.* Philadelphia: Presbyterian and Reformed, 1968 [1956].

Warfield, Benjamin B., *Calvin and Augustine.* Philadelphia: Presbyterian and Reformed, 1956.

Warfield, Benjamin B., *Calvin and Calvinism.* New York: Oxford University Press, 1931.

Warfield, Benjamin B., *Counterfeit Miracles.* Edinburgh: Banner of Truth, 1972 [1917].

Wileman, William, *John Calvin: His Life, His Teaching, and His Influence.*
 Choteau: Gospel Mission, 1981.
Williamson, G.I., *The Scriptural Regulative Principle of Worship.* Flat Rock:
 Bonclarken Assembly, 1990.
Young, Edward J., *Thy Word Is Truth.* Grand Rapids: Eerdmans, 1957.

SCRIPTURE INDEX

INDEX

Abraham, 55, 93
Academy, 12
Adam, 39, 48, 50-52, 55, 56, 71, 100
Adoption, 29, 77, 79
Adultery, 13
Against the Fantastic and Raging Sect of the Libertines (Calvin), 9
Alexander, J.H., 105; *Works: Ladies of the Reformation,* 105n11
Allegories, 28
Amillennialism, 102
Anabaptists, 3, 9, 110n24
Analogy of faith, 28
Angels, 40
Anglicanism, 95
Annihilationism, 100
Anselm, 68
Antichrist, 103
Antinomianism, 77
Antithesis, 110n12
Apollinarianism, 63
Apologetics, 19
Apostasy, 103

Apostles, 6, 19, 22, 65, 86, 109n11, 115n5
Apostles creed, 64, 66, 68, 85, 87
Apostolic Preaching of the Cross, The (Morris), 112n8, 114n16
Arianism, 63
Aristocracy, 11
Aristotle, 3
Arminianism, 73-74
Ascension of Christ, 64-66
Assent, 75
Assurance, 80-81
Atonement, 66-69
Atonement, The (Clark), 107n4
"Atonement: Sacrifice and Penalty, The" (Paul), 113n13
Attributes of God, 63
Augustine, 8, 16, 28, 36, 39, 43, 48, 50, 64, 83, 84, 85, 92, 108n8, 112n1
Author of evil, 43

Bahnsen, Greg, 110n12

THE CRISIS OF OUR TIME

Historians have christened the thirteenth century the Age of Faith and termed the eighteenth century the Age of Reason. The twentieth century has been called many things: the Atomic Age, the Age of Inflation, the Age of the Tyrant, the Age of Aquarius. But it deserves one name more than the others: the Age of Irrationalism. Contemporary secular intellectuals are anti-intellectual. Contemporary philosophers are anti-philosophy. Contemporary theologians are anti-theology.

In past centuries secular philosophers have generally believed that knowledge is possible to man. Consequently they expended a great deal of thought and effort trying to justify knowledge. In the twentieth century, however, the optimism of the secular philosophers has all but disappeared. They despair of knowledge.

Like their secular counterparts, the great theologians and doctors of the church taught that knowledge is possible to man. Yet the theologians of the twentieth century have repudiated that belief. They also despair of knowledge. This radical skepticism has filtered down from the philosophers and theologians and penetrated our entire culture, from television to music to literature. *The Christian in the twentieth century is confronted with an overwhelming cultural consensus—sometimes stated explicitly, but most often implicitly: Man does not and cannot know anything truly.*

What does this have to do with Christianity? Simply this: If man can know nothing truly, man can truly know nothing. We cannot know that the Bible is the Word of God, that Christ died for the sins of his people, or that Christ is alive today at the right hand of the Father. Unless knowledge is possible, Christianity is nonsensical, for it claims to be knowledge. What is at stake in the twentieth century is not simply a single doctrine, such as the Virgin Birth, or the existence of hell, as important as those doctrines may be, but the whole of Christianity itself. If knowledge is not possible to man, it is worse than silly to argue points of doctrine—it is insane.

The irrationalism of the present age is so thorough-going and pervasive that even the Remnant—the segment of the professing church that remains faithful—has accepted much of it, frequently without even being aware of what it was accepting. In some circles this irrationalism has become synonymous with piety and humility, and those who oppose it are denounced as rationalists—as though to be logical were a sin. Our contemporary anti-theologians make a contradiction and call it a Mystery. The faithful ask for truth and are given Paradox. If any balk at swallowing the absurdities of the anti-theologians, they are frequently marked as heretics or schismatics who seek to act independently of God.

There is no greater threat facing the true Church of Christ at this moment than the irrationalism that now controls our entire culture. Totalitarianism, guilty of tens of millions of murders, including those of millions of Christians, is to be feared, but not nearly so much as the idea that we do not and cannot know the truth. Hedonism, the popular philosophy of America, is not to be feared so much as the belief that logic—that "mere human logic," to use the religious irrationalists' own phrase—is futile. The attacks on truth, on revelation, on the intellect, and on logic are renewed daily. But note well: The misologists—the haters of logic—use logic to demonstrate the futility of using logic. The anti-intellectuals construct intricate intellectual arguments to prove the insufficiency of the intellect. The anti-theologians use the revealed Word of God to show that there can be no revealed Word of God—or that if there could, it would remain impenetrable darkness and Mystery to our finite minds.

Nonsense Has Come

Is it any wonder that the world is grasping at straws—the straws of experientialism, mysticism and drugs? After all, if people are told that the Bible contains insoluble mysteries, then is not a flight into mysticism to be expected? On what grounds can it be condemned? Certainly not on logical grounds or Biblical grounds, if logic is futile and the Bible unintelligible. Moreover, if it cannot be condemned on logical or Biblical grounds, it cannot be condemned at all. If people are going to have a religion of the mysterious, they will not adopt Christianity: They will have a genuine mystery religion. "Those who call for Nonsense," C.S. Lewis once wrote, "will find that it comes." And that is precisely what has happened. The popularity of Eastern mysticism, of drugs, and of religious experience is the logical consequence of the irrationalism of the twentieth century. There can and will be no Christian revival—and no reconstruction of society—unless and until the irrationalism of the age is totally repudiated by Christians.

The Church Defenseless

Yet how shall they do it? The spokesmen for Christianity have been fatally infected with irrationalism. The seminaries, which annually train thousands of men to teach millions of Christians, are the finishing schools of irrationalism, completing the job begun by the government schools and colleges. Some of the pulpits of the most conservative churches (we are not speaking of the apostate churches) are occupied by graduates of the anti-theological schools. These products of modern anti-theological education, when asked to give a reason for the hope that is in them, can generally respond with only the intellectual analogue of a shrug—a mumble about Mystery. They have not grasped—and therefore cannot teach those for whom they are responsible—the first truth: "And ye shall know the truth." Many, in fact, explicitly deny it, saying that, at best, we possess only "pointers" to the truth, or something "similar" to the truth, a mere analogy. Is the impotence of the Christian Church a puzzle? Is the fascination with pentecostalism and faith healing among members of conservative churches an enigma? Not when one understands the sort of studied nonsense that is purveyed in the name of God in the seminaries.

The Trinity Foundation

The creators of The Trinity Foundation firmly believe that theology is too important to be left to the licensed theologians —the graduates of the schools of theology. They have created The Trinity Foundation for the express purpose of teaching the faithful all that the Scriptures contain—not warmed over, baptized, secular philosophies. Each member of the board of directors of The Trinity Foundation has signed this oath: "I believe that the Bible alone and the Bible in its entirety is the Word of God and, therefore, inerrant in the autographs. I believe that the system of truth presented in the Bible is best summarized in the Westminster Confession of Faith. So help me God."

The ministry of The Trinity Foundation is the presentation of the system of truth taught in Scripture as clearly and as completely as possible. We do not regard obscurity as a virtue, nor confusion as a sign of spirituality. Confusion, like all error, is sin, and teaching that confusion is all that Christians can hope for is doubly sin.

The presentation of the truth of Scripture necessarily involves the rejection of error. The Foundation has exposed and will continue to expose the irrationalism of the twentieth century, whether its current spokesman be an existentialist philosopher or a professed Reformed theologian. We oppose anti-intellectualism, whether it be espoused by a neo-orthodox theologian or a fundamentalist evangelist. We reject misology, whether it be on the lips of a neo-evangelical or those of a Roman Catholic charismatic. To each error we bring the brilliant light of Scripture, proving all things, and holding fast to that which is true.

The Primacy of Theory

The ministry of The Trinity Foundation is not a "practical" ministry. If you are a pastor, we will not enlighten you on how to organize an ecumenical prayer meeting in your community or how to double church attendance in a year. If you are a homemaker, you will have to read elsewhere to find out how to become a total woman. If you are a businessman, we will not tell you how to develop a social conscience. The professing church is drowning in such "practical" advice.

The Trinity Foundation is unapologetically theoretical in its outlook, believing that theory without practice is dead, and that practice without theory is blind. The trouble with the professing church is not primarily in its practice, but in its theory. Christians do not know, and many do not even care to know, the doctrines of Scripture. Doctrine is intellectual, and Christians are generally anti-intellectual. Doctrine is ivory tower philosophy, and they scorn ivory towers. The ivory tower, however, is the control tower of a civilization. It is a fundamental, theoretical mistake of the practical men to think that they can be merely practical, for practice is always the practice of some theory. The relationship between theory and practice is the relationship between cause and effect. If a person believes correct theory, his practice will tend to be correct. The practice of contemporary Christians is immoral because it is the practice of false theories. It is a major theoretical mistake of the practical men to think that they can ignore the ivory towers of the philosophers and theologians as irrelevant to their lives. Every action that the "practical" men take is governed by the thinking that has occurred in some ivory tower—whether that tower be the British Museum, the Academy, a home in Basel, Switzerland, or a tent in Israel.

In Understanding Be Men

It is the first duty of the Christian to understand correct theory—correct doctrine—and thereby implement correct practice. This order—first theory, then practice—is both logical and Biblical. It is, for example, exhibited in Paul's epistle to the Romans, in which he spends the first eleven chapters expounding theory and the last five discussing practice. The contemporary teachers of Christians have not only reversed the order, they have inverted the Pauline emphasis on theory and practice. The virtually complete failure of the teachers of the professing church to instruct the faithful in correct doctrine is the cause of the misconduct and cultural impotence of Christians. The Church's lack of power is the result of its lack of truth. The *Gospel* is the power of God, not religious experience or personal relationship. The Church has no power because it has abandoned the Gospel, the good news, for a religion of experientialism. Twentieth century American Christians are children carried about by every wind of doctrine, not knowing what they believe, or even if they believe anything for certain.

The chief purpose of The Trinity Foundation is to counteract the irrationalism of the age and to expose the errors of the teachers of the church. Our emphasis—on the Bible as the sole source of truth, on the primacy of the intellect, on the supreme importance of correct doctrine, and on the necessity for systematic and logical thinking—is almost unique in Christendom. To the extent that the church survives—and she will survive and flourish—it will be because of her increasing acceptance of these basic ideas and their logical implications.

We believe that the Trinity Foundation is filling a vacuum in Christendom. We are saying that Christianity is intellectually defensible—that, in fact, it is the only intellectually defensible system of thought. We are saying that God has made the wisdom of this world—whether that wisdom be called science, religion, philosophy, or common sense—foolishness. We are appealing to all Christians who have not conceded defeat in the intellectual battle with the world to join us in our efforts to raise a standard to which all men of sound mind can repair.

The love of truth, of God's Word, has all but disappeared in our time. We are committed to and pray for a great instauration. But though we may not see this reformation of Christendom in our lifetimes, we believe it is our duty to present the whole counsel of God because Christ has commanded it. The results of our teaching are in God's hands, not ours. Whatever those results, his Word is never taught in vain, but always accomplishes the result that he intended it to accomplish. Professor Gordon H. Clark has stated our view well:

There have been times in the history of God's people, for example, in the days of Jeremiah, when refreshing grace and widespread revival were not to be expected: the time was one of chastisement. If this twentieth century is of a similar nature, individual Christians here and there can find comfort and strength in a study of God's Word. But if God has decreed happier days for us and if we may expect a world-shaking and genuine spiritual awakening, then it is the author's belief that a zeal for souls, however necessary, is not the sufficient condition. Have there not been devout saints in every age, numerous enough to carry on a revival? Twelve such persons are plenty. What distinguishes the arid ages from the period of the Reformation, when nations were moved as they had not been since Paul preached in Ephesus, Corinth, and Rome, is the latter's fullness of knowledge of God's Word. To echo an early Reformation thought, when the ploughman and the garage attendant know the Bible as well as the theologian does, and know it better than some contemporary theologians, then the desired awakening shall have already occurred.

In addition to publishing books, of which *What Calvin Says* is the thirty-fifth, the Foundation publishes a monthly newsletter, *The Trinity Review*. Subscriptions to *The Review* are free; please write to the address below to become a subscriber. If you would like further information or would like to join us in our work, please let us know.

The Trinity Foundation is a non-profit foundation tax-exempt under section 501 (c)(3) of the Internal Revenue Code of 1954. You can help us disseminate the Word of God through your tax-deductible contributions to the Foundation.

And we know that the Son of God is come, and hath given us an understanding, that we may know him that is true, and we are in him that is true, in his Son Jesus Christ. This is the true God, and eternal life.

John W. Robbins

INTELLECTUAL AMMUNITION

The Trinity Foundation is committed to the reconstruction of philosophy and theology along Biblical lines. We regard God's command to bring all our thoughts into conformity with Christ very seriously, and the books listed below are designed to accomplish that goal. They are written with two subordinate purposes: (1) to demolish all secular claims to knowledge; and (2) to build a system of truth based upon the Bible alone.

Philosophy

Behaviorism and Christianity, Gordon H. Clark $6.95
    Behaviorism *is a critique of both secular and religious behaviorists. It includes chapters on John Watson, Edgar S. Singer Jr., Gilbert Ryle, B.F. Skinner, and Donald MacKay. Clark's refutation of behaviorism and his argument for a Christian doctrine of man are unanswerable.*

A Christian Philosophy of Education, Gordon H. Clark $8.95
    The first edition of this book was published in 1946. It sparked the contemporary interest in Christian schools. Dr. Clark has thoroughly revised and updated it, and it is needed now more than ever. Its chapters include: The Need for a World-View, The Christian World-View, The Alternative to Christian Theism, Neutrality, Ethics, The Christian Philosophy of Education, Academic Matters, Kindergarten to University.

Three appendices are included as well: The Relationship of Public Education to Christianity, A Protestant World-View, and Art and the Gospel.

A Christian View of Men and Things, Gordon H. Clark $10.95
No other book achieves what A Christian View *does: the presentation of Christianity as it applies to history, politics, ethics, science, religion, and epistemology. Clark's command of both worldly philosophy and Scripture is evident on every page, and the result is a breathtaking and invigorating challenge to the wisdom of this world.*

Clark Speaks From The Grave, Gordon H. Clark $3.95
Dr. Clark chides some of his critics for their failure to defend Christianity competently. Clark Speaks *is a stimulating and illuminating discussion of the errors of contemporary apologists.*

Education, Christianity, and the State $7.95
J. Gresham Machen
Machen was one of the foremost educators, theologians, and defenders of Christianity in the twentieth century. The author of numerous scholarly books, Machen saw clearly that if Christianity is to survive and flourish, a system of Christian grade schools must be established. This collection of essays captures his thought on education over nearly three decades.

Essays on Ethics and Politics $10.95
Gordon H. Clark
Clark's s essays, written over the course of five decades, are a major statement of Christian ethics.

Gordon H. Clark: Personal Recollections $6.95
John W. Robbins, editor
Friends of Dr. Clark have written their recollections of the man. Contributors include family members, colleagues, students, and friends such as Harold Lindsell, Carl Henry, Ronald Nash, Dwight Zeller, and Mary Crumpacker. The book includes an extensive bibliography of Clark's work.

John Dewey, Gordon H. Clark $2.00

America has not produced many philosophers, but John Dewey has been extremely influential. Clark examines his philosophy of Instrumentalism.

Logic, Gordon H. Clark $8.95

Written as a textbook for Christian schools, Logic *is another unique book from Clark's pen. His presentation of the laws of thought, which must be followed if Scripture is to be understood correctly, and which are found in Scripture itself, is both clear and thorough.* Logic *is an indispensable book for the thinking Christian.*

The Philosophy of Science and Belief in God $5.95
Gordon H. Clark

In opposing the contemporary idolatry of science, Clark analyzes three major aspects of science: the problem of motion, Newtonian science, and modern theories of physics. His conclusion is that science, while it may be useful, is always false; and he demonstrates its falsity in numerous ways. Since science is always false, it can offer no objection to the Bible and Christianity.

Religion, Reason and Revelation, Gordon H. Clark $7.95

One of Clark's apologetical masterpieces, Religion, Reason and Revelation *has been praised for the clarity of its thought and language. It includes chapters on Is Christianity a Religion? Faith and Reason, Inspiration and Language, Revelation and Morality, and God and Evil. It is must reading for all serious Christians.*

Thales to Dewey: A History of Philosophy paper $11.95
Gordon H. Clark hardback $16.95

This volume is the best one volume history of philosophy in English.

Three Types of Religious Philosophy, Gordon H. Clark $6.95

In this book on apologetics, Clark examines empiricism, rationalism, dogmatism, and contemporary irrationalism, which does not rise to the level of philosophy. He offers a solution to the question, "How can Christianity be defended before the world?"

Theology

The Atonement, Gordon H. Clark $8.95

This is a major addition to Clark's multi-volume systematic theology. In The Atonement, *Clark discusses the Covenants, the Virgin Birth and Incarnation, federal headship and representation, the relationship between God's sovereignty and justice, and much more. He analyzes traditional views of the Atonement and criticizes them in the light of Scripture alone.*

The Biblical Doctrine of Man, Gordon H. Clark $6.95

Is man soul and body or soul, spirit, and body? What is the image of God? Is Adam's sin imputed to his children? Is evolution true? Are men totally depraved? What is the heart? These are some of the questions discussed and answered from Scripture in this book.

Cornelius Van Til: The Man and The Myth $2.45
John W. Robbins

The actual teachings of this eminent Philadelphia theologian have been obscured by the myths that surround him. This book penetrates those myths and criticizes Van Til's surprisingly unorthodox views of God and the Bible.

Faith and Saving Faith, Gordon H. Clark $6.95

The views of the Roman Catholic church, John Calvin, Thomas Manton, John Owen, Charles Hodge, and B.B. Warfield are discussed in this book. Is the object of faith a person or a proposition? Is faith more than belief? Is belief more than thinking with assent, as Augustine said? In a world chaotic with differing views of faith, Clark clearly explains the Biblical view of faith and saving faith.

God's Hammer: The Bible and Its Critics $6.95
Gordon H. Clark

The starting point of Christianity, the doctrine on which all other doctrines depend, is "The Bible alone is the Word of God written, and therefore inerrant in the autographs." Over the centuries the opponents of Christianity, with Satanic shrewdness, have concentrated their attacks on the truthfulness and completeness of the Bible. In the twentieth century the attack is not so much in the fields of history and archaeology as in philosophy. Clark's brilliant defense of the complete truthfulness of the Bible is captured in this collection of eleven major essays.

Guide to the Westminster Confession and Catechism $13.95
James E. Bordwine
This large book contains the full text of both the Westminster Confession (both original and American versions) and the Larger Catechism. In addition, it offers a chapter-by-chapter summary of the Confession and a unique index to both the Confession and the Catechism.

The Incarnation, Gordon H. Clark $8.95
Who was Christ? The attack on the Incarnation in the nineteenth and twentieth centuries has been vigorous, but the orthodox response has been lame. Clark reconstructs the doctrine of the Incarnation building and improving upon the Chalcedonian definition.

In Defense of Theology, Gordon H. Clark $9.95
There are four groups to whom Clark addresses this book: the average Christians who are uninterested in theology, the atheists and agnostics, the religious experientialists, and the serious Christians. The vindication of the knowledge of God against the objections of three of these groups is the first step in theology.

The Johannine Logos, Gordon H. Clark $5.95
Clark analyzes the relationship between Christ, who is the truth, and the Bible. He explains why John used the same word to refer to both Christ and his teaching. Chapters deal with the Prologue to John's Gospel, Logos and Rheemata, Truth, and Saving Faith.

Logical Criticisms of Textual Criticism $3.25
Gordon H. Clark
In this critique of the science of textual criticism, Dr. Clark exposes the fallacious argumentation of the modern textual critics and defends the view that the early Christians knew better than the modern critics which manuscripts of the New Testament were more accurate.

Pat Robertson: A Warning to America, John W. Robbins $6.95

The Protestant Reformation was based on the Biblical principle that the Bible is the only revelation from God, yet a growing religious movement, led by Pat Robertson, asserts that God speaks to them directly. This book addresses the serious issue of religious fanaticism in America by examining the theological views of Pat Robertson.

Predestination, Gordon H. Clark $8.95

Clark thoroughly discusses one of the most controversial and pervasive doctrines of the Bible: that God is, quite literally, Almighty. Free will, the origin of evil, God's omniscience, creation, and the new birth are all presented within a Scriptural framework. The objections of those who do not believe in the Almighty God are considered and refuted. This edition also contains the text of the booklet, Predestination in the Old Testament.

Sanctification, Gordon H. Clark $8.95

In this book, which is part of Clark's multi-volume systematic theology, he discusses historical theories of sanctification, the sacraments, and the Biblical doctrine of sanctification.

Scripture Twisting in the Seminaries. Part 1: Feminism $5.95
John W. Robbins

An analysis of the views of three graduates of Westminster Seminary on the role of women in the church.

Today's Evangelism: Counterfeit or Genuine? $6.95
Gordon H. Clark

Clark compares the methods and messages of today's evangelists with Scripture, and finds that Christianity is on the wane because the Gospel has been distorted or lost. This is an extremely useful and enlightening book.

The Trinity, Gordon H. Clark $8.95

Apart from the doctrine of Scripture, no teaching of the Bible is more important than the doctrine of God. Clark's defense of the orthodox doctrine of the Trinity is a principal portion of a major new work of Systematic Theology now in progress. There are chapters on the deity of Christ, Augustine, the incomprehensibility of God, Bavinck and Van Til, and the Holy Spirit, among others.

What Calvin Says, W. Gary Crampton $7.95
     This book is an introduction to the theology of one of the world's greatest theologians, John Calvin. Its ten chapters cover all the major topics of theology, from Scripture to the last things. An appendix on the five points of Calvinism and two indexes complete the book.

What Do Presbyterians Believe? Gordon H. Clark $7.95
     This classic introduction to Christian doctrine has been republished. It is the best commentary on the Westminster Confession of Faith that has ever been written.

Commentaries on the New Testament

Colossians, Gordon H. Clark $6.95
Ephesians, Gordon H. Clark $8.95
First Corinthians, Gordon H. Clark $10.95
First John, Gordon H. Clark $10.95
First and Second Thessalonians, Gordon H. Clark $5.95
The Pastoral Epistles (I and II Timothy and Titus) $9.95
     Gordon H. Clark
     All of Clark's commentaries are expository, not technical, and are written for the Christian layman. His purpose is to explain the text clearly and accurately so that the Word of God will be thoroughly known by every Christian.

The Trinity Library

We will send you one copy of each of the 37 books listed above for the low price of $200. The regular price of these books is $282.50. You may also order the books you want individually on the order blank on the next page. Because some of the books are in short supply, we must reserve the right to substitute others of equal or greater value in The Trinity Library. This special offer expires June 30, 1995.